The Skooter Travels the World
in Search of Adventure

Dear Publiana,
    Many thanks for all your
wonderful care- both for Mrs. D
and me !! You are terrific !!!
    God Bless
        Dave D.

The Skooter Travels the World

In Search of Adventure

David C. Dressler

Dudley Court Press
Sonoita, Arizona

Published in the United States of America by
Dudley Court Press
PO Box 102
Sonoita, AZ 85637
www.DudleyCourtPress.com
520-329-2729

ISBN: 9781940013169

Printed in the USA

Contents

Prologue

I was raised in Cleveland, Ohio, a solid mid-western industrial city. I wanted to leave to "spread my wings" but really did not know exactly what that meant.

At the end of high school I met an amazing, attractive young woman named Skooter who had more energy and vitality than anyone I have ever known. But how did that fit with my desire to spread my wings and leave Cleveland?

Yale helped broaden me. And after several years of an up and down romance with The Skooter, in the summer of 1949, I put her to a test. At an exquisite dinner dance in Washington, DC at the Columbia Country Club, I asked, if we were ever to consider getting married, would she move to California with me? (At least it was out of Cleveland). She said yes.

Actually this cute, energetic young girl had lots of eligible suitors pursuing her so I wasn't even sure why she wanted me (I considered myself to be pretty dull) but for some reason, she did.

Then came graduation from Yale in 1950 and suddenly a war in Korea beckoned. I was in the Marine Corps Reserves so it was certain I would face a call-up—not the kind of adventure I might want to seek.

I went to Cleveland in July of 1950 and took The Skooter to the Cleveland Indians-Detroit Tigers Saturday afternoon baseball game. Previously we had talked about possibly getting a ring but I kept mum during the whole game, to her obvious consternation. Eventually the game ended with the Indians winning, and I said something about the ring. Somehow we got downtown before the stores closed at 5:00 p.m. and I discovered she had a ring all picked out. So I learned she was a "doer and a planner". I spent all the money I had—literally—so we started marriage in December of 1950 with zero cash but lots of love.

Since we were so young I felt it would be difficult to introduce my new bride as Skooter so she started calling herself Dee. My mistake; she was nicknamed Skooter when she started crawling as a baby. She kept on "skooting" thru life everywhere she went.

This book is dedicated to the memory of the wonderful woman with whom I enjoyed sixty terrific years of as happy a marriage as one could have. In this book she is called "The Skooter," a unique title for a unique person seeking unique adventures all over the world.

Introduction

The world is a fascinating place to explore! Today it is easier than ever to undertake that exploration as an individual and fully enjoy it. But certain cautions, important in the past, are even more important now. This book is dedicated to helping the average person pick the delightful spots they can explore on their own and enjoy in relative peace and tranquility at their own pace.

Love is what glues the world together, but we must bear in mind that historically the world has had almost constant wars and insurrections, and those have left deep scars on its people, who individually are loving and friendly. Scratch those scars and there is bleeding again.

I have always said [based on my experiences] that people worldwide are inherently good and friendly, but there are bad governments and leaders who lead the people astray. But that should not prevent individuals, as travelers and explorers, from enjoying all that the world has to offer in whatever way they may choose.

The travel "bug" didn't hit The Skooter and me until later in life since we were busy raising kids and trying to get a financial toe-hold. Since I worked for, and eventually became president of a company that did more than half its sales outside the US (which was unusual at that time), my immersion in the world abroad was a necessity. Once The

Skooter started traveling, she was incurable. She traveled with me on business as often as she could (which was much more common in those days) and took every possible break or vacation to explore some of the remotest spots in the world in search of adventure or just plain fun. And adventure we did find!

Bear in mind that all these chapters are snapshots in time. While some things in the world don't change, others change rapidly and not always for the better, so pick your travel destinations carefully. Some of the places covered in this book I would not go back to at this time. All stories are true.

The Skooter's friends often used the word "fearless" in describing her approach to the ends of the world, but she never got in big trouble. Maybe her love of people, as well as animals, just radiated and kept her safe.

I always said she had a guardian angel on each shoulder.

Chapter 1

An African Dictator
Face to Face

It all starts with a small inheritance from Aunt Grace.
The Skooter says we have to go to Africa, so there we go: British Airways
from London to Kampala, Uganda (Entebbe Airport). So far so good,
but upon landing and arrival at baggage, we find that British Airways
has lost 3 of our 4 bags. Furthermore, no BA agent present at the airport
could write so I have to stay behind to fill out the lost baggage forms.

On to the hotel and dinner, but the place is loaded with military
security. Being curious, we have to try to find out what is going on to attract all the attention. There is a big party and The Skooter never wanted
to miss a party so we go to the door where we found guards armed
with AK-47's blocking our way. A very large jovial black man is obvi-

ously being deferred to as the life of the party. He waives us in past the guards. There is a program of dancers from Swaziland and cocktails and appetizers.

It is a diplomatic reception given by the leader (dictator) of Uganda, Idi Amin. The Skooter takes a picture of me with Idi looking like old buddies. All the diplomats from all over the world are there and it is a fun party. Idi is a lively dancer and very gregarious.

British Airways gives me the grand sum of $25.00 to buy some clothes (for my 2 lost bags) so I shop in downtown Kampala for some khaki trousers that are about mid-calf length (Ugandans were short). They wore like iron and became my life-long gardening trousers.

We soon find we are in a land of dictatorship. Over time in our later travels we also find that this is not so rare. Functioning democracies are in the minority around the world. A guide takes us to see Uganda's parliament building. She shows us where the opposition sits, but then adds, "Of course we have no opposition."

We head north with the objective of visiting the sources of the Nile River in northern Uganda and seeing wild animals. We see a dead native lying by the side of the road. Being very curious, we investigate. It turns out that he had found his friend, who had too much to drink, sleeping by the side of the road with his bike. Fearing that the bike would be stolen he tried to take it home for safe-keeping. Other natives thought he was stealing the bike so they beat him to death. We are told it is the local system of "instant justice".

Our first night's sleep in the north is interrupted by laughing hyenas. Yes, they do sound like they are laughing. They are pack animals that can be vicious killers so I never much liked them.

We drive by herds of elephants that are literally devastating the forest by stripping the bark off trees. Some parts of Africa have totally lost their elephants, but others suffer from over-population. Controlling the herds is a necessity.

We view the headwaters of the mighty Nile and beautiful Murchison Falls. The whole area is teeming with wildlife. More crocodiles than any place we ever visit! They are big and seemingly hungry and they surround our little boat. And lots of hippopotamuses that, we are told, kill more tourists than any other wild animal in Africa.

We go back to our lodge after our day on our little boat. Our room has two doors. When it's time for us to take the short walk to dinner, I open the door to find a rampaging elephant throwing the porch furniture around with his trunk. Wrong choice! Close that door and go out the other door.

Around the corner of the building, we literally bump into a hippo that had come out of the river to graze on the good green grass around the lodge. Startled the heck out of us, but the hippo is intent on the grass, not us.

We make it back to Entebbe, but I have become very sick with diarrhea. Lesson learned. Remote places in the world lack refrigeration so intestinal bugs abound and thrive. Bring along your own medicine and eat cooked foods.

Entebbe airport has only a few hard wooden benches and a primitive toilet. Somehow I make it on the plane to Nairobi, Kenya and a decent hotel. The Skooter calls the house doctor. Soon there is a knock on out hotel door; a nurse in a white starched uniform announces to a startled Skooter that she has "come to take Mr. Dressler to surgery." The

Skooter protests that no "surgery" is planned. It is just the British way of saying I am going to the doctor's office.

Idi Amin turned out to be an erratic despot who killed 300,000 of his own people. In late June of 1976, he allowed a hijacked Air France plane to land at Entebbe and subsequently let all the non-Jews be released. But he kept over 100 Jews in the little Entebbe airport as hostages under deplorable conditions. On July 4, 1976, the Israel Defense Forces came over 2500 miles and made a successful rescue. The movie, *The Delta Force*, was made of this remarkable rescue. To this day, I have great empathy for the hostages who survived the hard benches and inadequate toilets and other atrocious conditions at Entebbe Airport, Uganda.

Idi Amin had an 8-year reign of terror in Uganda. Eventually in 1979, Ugandan exiles and Tanzanian troops combined to drive him out, but he survived and lived out his days in exile in Saudi Arabia. An excellent movie, *The Rise and Fall of Idi Amin*, was made on his reign of terror.

Uganda was ruined but it has come back. Murchison Falls, the headwaters of the Nile, and the mountain gorillas are worthy tourist attractions. (The Skooter chooses Rwanda, because of Dian Fossey, for us to pursue the mountain gorillas, largest of the great ape family – and this story is told in Chapter 3.)

Chapter 2

Avoiding "Rocks" on the Zambezi River

The Skooter decides to sign up for a canoeing and camping trip on the Zambezi River leading to Victoria Falls in Africa. I have told her I will go anywhere in the world with her as long as there is a comfortable and safe bed at the end of the day. This hardly qualifies. The Zambezi in Zimbabwe is a mighty river, and lions, elephants, and other wild animals use it as their watering hole. But I agree to go.

I haven't been in a canoe since I was a camp counselor in Maine as a teen-ager. We try a practice session in a swamp in Florida loaded with alligators. It is shaky but we stay afloat and don't tip over. Shooting the rapids on the Zambezi will be much more difficult and I am fearful. Not the Skooter—it's an adventure!

We arrive at the base camp on the Zambezi early in the morning and there is good news and bad news. The good news is that the overnight camping has been scratched (perhaps the wild animals became too intrusive for safe camping?). The bad news, for me, is that the canoes have now become two-man kayaks. I have never even been in a kayak, let alone shooting rapids. In Africa, expect the unexpected!

We sign forms absolving the tour company of any responsibility for injury or death. There are no helmets, four kayaks, a guide (from Minnesota) and two natives in a rubber raft, presumably to fish us out if we fall in the river. The other six participants are all much younger: four Aussies and two Germans. The Skooter and I make a strategic decision. We split up with the Germans but by chance she gets the young German who has kayaked before and I get the one who hasn't.

We are off through the rapids: lots of rocks and fast flowing water, and the occasional big pool of calm water with big rocks we are careful to avoid. But wait, those aren't rocks, they are hippos and they are not as peaceful as they look. They are huge and dangerous! Yes, we try to avoid them.

We also paddle near the shore and see the elephants that have come to drink up close and personal. It is a beautiful sight! We are told they will not charge us in the water. They trumpet but only make a few mock charges to try to tell to keep our distance.

Miraculously, we get through all the rapids without any of the kayaks "wiping out". Our guide seems disappointed, as if this is a first. So he tells us, "Since you have all done so well, I am going to teach you how to cross a rapid." This, of course, is infinitely harder. You have to try to gently edge the nose of the kayak into the flow of the current, which can be very strong.

Somehow my German and I go first. We are wearing life jackets and are instructed that if we tip over, "Just pull open the velcro holding

you in the kayak and you will eventually rise to the surface of the river." Emphasis on the "eventually". They could have added, "Provided you don't hit your head on a rock or run into a hippo, etc."

The strong current turns out to be more than we can handle and flips us over. I feel like I am headed to the bottom of the fast moving Zambezi — with no helmet. Fortunately, I encounter no rocks and eventually do come up, gasping for air. We are not going to be swept over Victoria Falls because the men in the rubber raft manage to head us off with great expertise and pull us into the raft. We find out later that swimming in the Zambezi is not recommended because of all the strange water creatures, including a very invasive worm.

Our guide apparently decides that this is all too dangerous, and the other kayaks do not make the attempt. The Skooter is frustrated that she never gets a chance to show her superior kayaking skills or be dunked in the Zambezi. We reach shore and eat a late lunch. I am very wet but delighted to be alive. Never again will I attempt to kayak rapids. I am a retired kayaker!

We spend some time at Victoria Falls, which is a magnificent sight when the water is flowing fully. There are flimsy or no railings, so walking around on the slippery paths takes care. We stay at the Victoria Falls Hotel, which seems like it is part of a revival of the old British Empire.

Outside, the grounds are stunning with the sound and mist of Victoria Falls in the background. Inside, everywhere, there are antique posters depicting the role of each country in the British Empire. Fascinating bit of history!

At the bottom of Victoria Falls there are some pretty rugged rapids that you can raft through, but we are not even tempted. We decide to walk across the bridge to Zambia. We are told not to bring valuables, and to be careful. At the end of the bridge, there are Zambian soldiers who demand $100 when they see our passports. Since we don't have $100, we cannot enter, but I don't think we would have paid in any event.

Zimbabwe used to be called Rhodesia. The capital is Harare, which we visit. The country has rich farmlands and interesting parks, but, unfortunately, another dictator, Mugabe, has somehow survived a long time while completely ruining the country. He broke up the productive farms and chased out their legal owners. Squatters and small subsistence farmers were an unsuccessful replacement. Inflation kept rising until the currency was worthless. Mugabe switched to the U.S. dollar but somehow he continues (illegally his foes say) to win elections while the country deteriorates.

NOTE:

About 2 years later I am reading the Sunday Washington Post at home and I see that two guides on the Zambezi have been eaten by a rogue hippo. One guide is dead and the other somehow extracted himself from the hippo's mouth, but without his arm, which the hippo ripped off at the shoulder. The guide is medivacked out by helicopter and apparently his life was saved. I tell The Skooter, "That is our cocky Zambezi guide from Minnesota." She doesn't believe me and rushes to her photo book. It is our guide! The hippos decided they had one too many invasions of their territory.

Chapter 3

The Elusive Mountain Gorilla

The Skooter is enthralled with what Dian Fossey has done with mountain gorillas, the elusive, huge apes inhabiting the Mountains of the Mist, the Virunga Mountains in Rwanda. So we are off to Kigali, the capital of Rwanda, a small, heavily populated mountainous country in central Africa, ruled in an uneasy coalition by two tribes who hate each other, the Hutus and Tutsis. Only three flights a week access Kilgali from Nairobi, in neighboring Kenya.

We almost miss our flight because we can't get a taxi from our lodge. We are at the lodge because our arrangements for the night in Nairobi hadn't materialized. None of the phones at the airport work. We get on the plane by using a couple large tips to encourage slow-moving airline employees. The perils of traveling alone in strange continents! Allow time for the unexpected.

Rwanda was formerly part of a Belgian colony and everyone speaks French. Our hotel is modest in downtown Kilgali, which looks rather run-down. Arrangements have been made for a small car and driver through a local travel agent.

It is Sunday, but The Skooter says we can't just sit around the hotel, so we take a walk to the local marketplace, where we stand out as some sort of oddity. Unfortunately, as we are walking around the market, The Skooter steps into an open drainage ditch and twists her ankle. She limps back to the hotel and wants me to get her some ice. Easier said than done. I don't know the French word for "ice" but through some good sign language, I eventually prevail at the bar.

I am concerned that we have come all this way to climb mountains to see gorillas and it will all be aborted. But miraculously the next morning The Skooter feels better. Our driver Maurice arrives and we are off for the Virunga Mountains and the gorillas. This all takes some advance planning since you must obtain tickets well ahead of time and the number sold is strictly limited. Dian Fossey opposed tourism because she felt that the gorillas were too susceptible to human illnesses. So anyone sick, or looking sick, is not supposed to go on the trek.

Our group assembles very early in the morning and consists of eight people with two official park guides. There are also numerous independent porters who tag along to carry cameras or whatever for a dollar or two. On the slow rise in the beginning of the climb, we pass some small farms and natives. Rwanda has lots of people and not much good farmland. The people subsist on a diet heavy on potatoes.

Our guides' first objective is to find where the gorilla group spent the last night, since they change nesting spots every night. The climb gets steeper and the terrain more rugged. The bamboo is relatively easy to get through, but much thicker vegetation and "stinging nettles" require the guides to use their machetes. It is a difficult climb, but around noon we see a phenomenal sight! A huge "silver-back" (called that because of the streak of silver hair running down his back) is crouching, transfixed and staring at something very intently. He must weigh 450 lbs. and looks in great shape (wouldn't the Washington Redskins love to have him on their line, I wonder). We get within about 20 yards of him and all cameras are clicking, but he is paying no attention to us.

The guides maneuver us around this fantastic sight. It turns out he is scouting the gorilla troop we have come to observe because he is planning to attack the leader that night and take over the group. Mountain gorillas live in small groups with a dominant male, a number of females,

and numerous offspring. At a certain age, the young males get kicked out and have to go out on their own as bachelors until they can challenge a leader, fight, win, and take over. Our guy doing the scouting is old enough, big enough, and fit enough to challenge. That night he will.

We find the group around noon. They have had lunch: bamboo sprouts and whatever. Now the females want to take a siesta but the little ones are just like human kids, full of life and teasing mom, who brushes them off brusquely, because they are interrupting her nap. The kids are fascinated by us, staring intently with those big brown eyes. We have been instructed not to make direct eye contact, make no sudden movements, and don't get too close. All of this goes out the window with these little ones who stare at us, get within a yard or two, as close as they can, and do everything but initiate a conversation. The cameras click endlessly. The guides have sticks they use skillfully to prevent close direct contact and actually do grunting sounds that imitate those of the gorillas. What an experience!

After about an hour of face-to-face contact, we are told that we have to leave, reluctantly of course. We hike a ways and then find a spot to sit and relax. One of our fellow hikers picks the wrong spot to sit—an anthill. Soon he is howling and jumping around with ants in the pants—literally.

The downward trek is easier. We see a Cape buffalo up close but otherwise it is uneventful until The Skooter spots a group of Hutu soldiers in training and decides, unwisely, that they would make a good video. They don't agree. There is an eruption and some of the soldiers charge her shaking their fists. The whole country seems on edge. It is.

The next day we start another trek up the mountains in search of another gorilla group. But this time it is easier and we encounter them at a lower altitude. The guides explain to us that we are very fortunate. The gorilla leader led the group to a lower altitude because one of the females

was giving birth that night. So there she is, a new mother with an hours-old baby gorilla nestled in her breasts, nursing. What a loving and caring sight!

Normally the most danger one can be in with wild animals anywhere is when a mother is with her young whom she wants to protect. But this mother is amazingly calm. And daddy doesn't seem overly protective either so we have some fabulous gorilla family viewing and pictures before we had to leave.

We did learn from another viewing group later that they had seen the gorilla "challenger" we saw the previous day and he had lost the battle with the other gorilla for leadership of the group. Unbelievable! He was badly beaten up but still alive, so it had not been a battle to the death.

That night is our last in Rwanda. We had previously been to a game park near the border

with Uganda where we were told that the Tutsis were training and massing for an attack on the Hutus in Rwanda, so we are anxious to make our flight out before it all erupts.

Unfortunately, after our guide and driver Maurice dropped us at the hotel, he apparently decided to cross the border into The Congo — for what reason we will never know. Anyway, the next morning we are packed and ready to go, but no Maurice. Not being able to communicate with anyone, we are in somewhat of a panic. But a lovely French lady appears out of nowhere and helps. She owns a flower plantation nearby.

Eventually, some policemen show up. Although they don't speak English they use sign language and imitate jail bars and say "Maurice kaput". Apparently Maurice is in jail in The Congo and won't be coming.

The nice French lady helps us telephone our travel agent in Kilgali and he says he will get us a taxi to the airport. We wait and wait, and finally a beat-up old car shows up with the driver stripped to the waist. For us, he puts on a shirt and off we go. We barely make our flight, which is full as they all are, as some wise people are intent on getting out.

Not long after, the Hutus and Tutsis went at it in one of the worst genocides the modern world has known. None of the Western powers or Africans intervened. Later a movie was made of all the slaughter and the brave people who tried to save innocent lives. I cannot help but wonder what happened to all the wonderful people we met in Rwanda, whether they were Hutus, Tutsis, Belgians, or French.

Chapter 4

Polar Bear Jail

The Skooter likes big, wild animals to photograph. Polar bear males weigh between 800-1,500 pounds and females about one-half that size. The scientific name translates to "sea bear." The polar bear is the only bear that is a marine mammal.

The Skooter discovers that Churchill, Manitoba, Canada is the polar bear capital of the world, so we must go. To get to Churchill, we fly to Winnipeg and then take the train to Churchill, which is located on the shores of Hudson Bay.

The two choices of where you stay are in a motel in downtown Churchill or in makeshift quarters out in the tundra, where you are immersed in polar bears 24 hours a day. We choose to stay downtown and make the daily trips in large vehicles, which are called dune buggies or tundra buggies. Actually these vehicles are quite comfortable and provide great viewing and photographing opportunities of the bears. The vehicles have large windows that open, and access doors at each end. It is important to have the

windows closed when the bears come up to the vehicle, out of curiosity or hunger. These bears have been hibernating all summer. The mothers have given birth to little ones and, of course, they are being nursed. so that makes mom even more eager to eat some solid food and not just live off stored fat.

The bears are waiting for Hudson Bay to start freezing over in the fall so they can go out on the ice and catch seals, which are their main diet all winter. It is a fascinating sight: mothers and cubs, huge males practicing their martial skills by "play fighting" to while away the time, and all looking for food. The bears are interested in us, particularly if they smell food. We have lunch every day on the vehicle and, of course, are instructed not to try to feed any leftovers to the bears.

We are usually out with the bears from dawn to dusk. We get lots of photos from various observation points since the vehicles are constantly moved around. Usually we are back in Churchill by nightfall. One late afternoon, we don't head back but head further out on the tundra as it gets dark. We are on a rescue mission for a broken-down vehicle. We arrive, and after much consultation, the men in charge decide they have to change the tires. They have a blow-torch and tools, but so much ice has accumulated on the wheels that they can't even get the lugs off. It is now very dark and I am worried: where are those hungry bears and wouldn't they like one of those guys for dinner? A bear could easily sneak up in the darkness, but fortunately it doesn't happen. Anyway, the men decide they can't make repairs and have to leave the vehicle there overnight. So we take their passengers and head back to Churchill.

Downtown Churchill is small and we are told not to walk around outside after dark. Why? Well, it seems that hungry bears wander into Churchill all the time looking for a meal. This has become such a hazard that Churchill has a special jail for polar bears. Unfortunately, the jail gets filled to capacity with captured bears and then what? They developed a unique system for strapping a polar bear or two to the bottom of a helicopter. The bears are airlifted 100 miles or so out of town and released.

Imagine if you were a hungry polar bear and you wandered into town looking for a meal and then, all of a sudden, you were captured and put in a strange jail. Then the next thing you know, you are in a sling, flying through the air to some strange place where you are abandoned—still very hungry.

Amazingly, they say most of the bears make it back to Churchill with maybe a stop at a house or dump for a snack. I never did learn whether Polar Bear Jail operated on a LIFO (last in-first out) or a FIFO (first in-first out) basis (joke for accountants).

Every year Hudson Bay eventually freezes over and the bears disappear out on the ice seeking seals. Of course global warming is a threat. What will the polar bears do if Hudson Bay doesn't freeze? My bet is, if the change comes slowly enough, these magnificent "sea bears" will find a way to adapt and survive. At least that is my fervent hope!

Chapter 5

Moses and the Burning Bush at Mt. Hebron

As The Skooter and I traveled the world, we were awed by the many fantastic places of worship that mankind has built, and the amount of human and physical capital that went into construction during times when the people's needs were great. Spiritual needs certainly rank high! Whether Christian churches in Western Europe, mosques all over the world, temples in India or Indonesia, Buddhist temples in Central Asia, they are all old and well worth visiting.

Some favorites we loved include Kyoto in Japan; the golden Buddha in Rangoon, Burma; the Blue Mosque in Istanbul; the Great Pyramid and

Mount Hebron

Luxor in Egypt; the huge new mosque in Abu Dhabi; and, of course, Notre Dame Cathedral in Paris. Every time we were in Paris, we went to Notre Dame to be spiritually refreshed. The stained glass windows, the massive structure of stone, the gargoyles — it's all just so impressive and spiritually satisfying.

All these places are easily accessible, but The Skooter and I set off for a place in a very remote location that proved an overwhelming surprise. In the 6th century, the Roman emperor, Justinian, constructed the walled stone monastery of St. Catherine in the Sinai in his desire to protect the monks living there. Monks still live there.

Camels were, of course, the old preferred way of transportation. We had tried camel riding in various places, mostly North Africa. They are an uncomfortable ride and this book does not have a chapter on camel adventures.

We settle on a van to get to St. Catherine's. The van crosses the vast

Sinai desert. It seems like endless miles of nothingness. Totally flat, hot, and lots of sand, but little or no vegetation. We are told that Moses and his followers wandered this desert for over 40 years. Suddenly, we come upon a view of Mt. Hebron, also called Mt. Sinai, rising out of the desert. The temperature cools as we climb. And it is green! There are trees of various varieties, including olive trees. There are bells and sheep and people. Bedouin tribesmen have lived around St. Catherine's since the time when the monastery was built.

It all seems like a paradise miraculously rising out of the desert. For Moses, after so many years wandering around the desert, it must have really seemed like a true miracle. The monks are scurrying around everywhere. Since we have escaped the desert heat, human activity

Above: Moses Well   Right: The Burning Bush at St. Catherine's

seems brisker. We get an American monk as a guide, and he is excellent. He guides us around the grounds and the library, which has some of the oldest books known to mankind.

And then, there it is! The Burning Bush where Moses received the Ten Commandments from God. The bush is very large and most impressive. Could it be that this bush has survived all these years? With no explanation to break the mood, it is easy to visualize Moses at this very bush talking to God. Awe-inspiring! The Skooter and I are great admirers of the Ten Commandments as one of the simplest and best ethics codes ever written. If only more people lived by them!

We walk around, absorbing as much as we can of this incredible atmosphere before leaving. St. Catherine's has continuously operated since it was built. Never involved in wars or fighting, it has been preserved. Hopefully it will continue to survive. Getting there is truly difficult and maybe a little dangerous, but it was really one of the most moving religious experiences we have had in our lives. By the time we departed, we felt more spiritually refreshed than ever before.

Chapter 6

Dinner with God in Guatemala

One night, The Skooter and I are having dinner at the Danish Embassy in Washington, D.C. She is absent from the dinner table but suddenly comes rushing back. Excitedly, she proclaims that she has "won" a trip to Guatemala.

It is very common for embassy dinners to have trips and other items available for a silent auction to the highest bidder, and often they are wonderful trips at bargain prices. But this is not a trip to terrific, civilized Denmark (we did go there and loved it), but a trip to Guatemala. I remind The Skooter that there is a revolution going on in Guatemala and people are getting killed, including tourists. I also remind her that she probably won because nobody else bid on the trip. She doesn't appreciate that undiplomatic remark and insists we are going because it will be an adventure.

Because I had learned from past experiences, I do some checking on the trip. I call the woman who donated it. She says it is all so beautiful, that if she "died there it would be okay". I tell The Skooter that I am not ready to die in Guatemala, at Lake Atitlan or anywhere. Somewhere The Skooter had heard that Lord Byron had said that Lake Atitlan is the most beautiful lake in the world. My guide book says it is the deepest lake in Central America, but also that there are no sewage plants — so raw sewage rolls down the streets of Panajachel, right into the lake.

I can't convince The Skooter that going to Guatemala is not the best trip to be taking in the midst of an active revolution, but I do manage to change the hotel reservations in Antigua to what sounds like a very interesting place, a monastery originally built by the Spanish and now being converted to a hotel. So we are off.

Antigua

We visit the Mayan Pyramids at Tikal in the middle of the jungle and find them well preserved and worth climbing around. So do the monkeys but they also like the trees. From Tikal we try to bypass Guatemala City by taking a taxi directly to Antigua, the ancient Spanish capital built in 1543.

We are unprepared for the total splendor of the lobby of our rebuilt monastery in Antigua. The long entrance walkway is lined with candles and silver. It is stunning and sparkling! The check-in desk is lined across the front with silver. Everywhere silver and more candles! No electric lights! In the midst of all this splendor is a courtyard and garden. I am thinking that this will be a heavenly place to "hangout" for a relaxing couple of days. But The Skooter is planning to go to Lake Atitlan, by bus no less—four hours out into the mountains and four hours back—with or without me.

I tell her she shouldn't go and try to talk her out of it. I don't like eight-hour public bus rides in third-world countries in war zones. I could have hired a car and driver for her, but I really thought I had convinced her not to go. The next morning when I wake up, she is gone. All day I feel guilty for not protecting her and hoping and praying nothing bad happens.

The Skooter returns that evening all aglow, but very tired, and tells me her story. She got off the bus in Panajachel after a long ride, walked to the beach where she had to find a boat to cross the lake where the Mayan women had a market selling their hand-made embroideries and tapestries. Not knowing how to get a boat, and not speaking Spanish, she had a challenge. She found a man on the beach in a white suit and tie, and she trusted him to help her. Her instincts must have been right again because she made it across the lake, bought what she described as fabulous fabrics (with designs of African animals that these women had never ever seen) and spent all her money. She made it back to Panajachel and luckily found a bus back to Antigua.

The hotel, in addition to silver and candles everywhere, has many antique religious statues that must have come from old Spanish churches. We run into them up and down the hall on the way to the dining room,

glowing in candlelight. The exhausted Skooter and a very relieved husband are seated in a small alcove right next to the largest, most impressive statue of all. He hovers over us. I finally ask the waiter just who that statue is. He replies, "GOD." So the three of us — The Skooter, husband, and God — have a very relaxed and excellent dinner. Actually, I felt God had been guiding her all day through her adventure.

We walk all around the charming colonial town of Antigua during the next couple of days. We visit the Chocolatela and, as chocolate lovers, learn how the Mayans made it. Antigua has suffered many earthquakes and subsequent rebuilding, but still retains that ancient Spanish colonial charm.

No revolutionaries attacked us. It is only when we get home that we read in the newspaper how they pulled a group of nuns off a bus on the way to Lake Atitlan, and killed them for some unknown reason.

The Skooter used the fabrics she brought back to cover an antique chair, and had some pillows made. Her only regret was that she hadn't taken more money on the bus so she could have bought more unique fabrics. The man in the white suit and tie on the beach, whom I would have been very suspicious of, guided her well. He had told her young boatmen to watch over her every minute and apparently they did.

Chapter 7

Lions Can Eat People

The Skooter and I loved lions. We saw and photographed lots of them on our many trips to Africa. Our first experience with lions was in Kenya, which has many terrific game parks. Lions live in prides with a dominant male, several mature females, and youngsters including cubs. The dominant males seem to have a good life. They are beautiful animals with large black or dark brown manes. The females seem to take good care of the male, since they do most of the hunting, deftly coordinating their efforts; raise the youngsters; and generally maintain order. The males seem to spend a lot of time lying around looking very regal. When the females make a "kill" the male gets the first crack at what he wants to eat. The good life may not last too long for the dominant male, however, because there are always young males out there who would like to take over.

Tanzania, adjacent to Kenya, is another great spot to see lions. The Serengeti National Park covers 5,600 square miles and abuts Kenya's Mara Masai Game Reserve. In the Serengeti's open plains exist a spectacular concentration of game animals, which the lions can feast on. Around April or May, there is a remarkable migration westward, which is well worth seeing, and provides many a tasty meal for all the carnivores along the way.

In East Africa at this time, most big game viewing was done by

Cape buffalo

riding in vans. The van drivers searched for lion prides and when one was found, all the vehicles congregated, each jockeying for the best viewing position. We visited Lake Manyara National Park in Tanzania to have a unique experience seeing lions that live in trees. Alas, a whole day and not even one lion. There is probably no worse travel experience than going a long way to view a particular wild animal and then coming up empty.

The Skooter decides on one of our many Africa trips that we should do something more exciting—a walking safari to give the animals a better look at us. So we hire a guide and the three of us take off, walking over terrain he selects. We flush out a warthog from his hole in the ground and he scares the h___ out of me, but charges off in the opposite direction.

Our guide carries a single-shot rifle and a pistol strapped to his waist. I ask him if he has ever been charged and he replies "Oh yes, many times. Once by a Cape buffalo, and I shot him right between the eyes, but he kept right on charging and gored me good. But the lion is the cleverest.

He weaves as he charges—that is why I have the pistol—-so if I miss my shot and he gets you, I can still save you. But don't run or you are finished."

On our walking safari we do see some elephants from a distance. Our guide tells us that the biggest danger is a mother with a youngster whom she is protecting, or a rogue or old animal that is hungry. However, we have no dangerous encounters on our long trek. We stay at a camp consisting of individual small huts on the edge of a jungle thicket that has, what looks like, a very inadequate fence. It turns out that just a few days before, the fence was very inadequate.

The huts are of course not air-conditioned and are stifling hot. Two men were staying in the hut and it was so hot, they decided to sleep on benches outside. During the night, a lion got over the fence and ate one of the men. It was explained that the lion was hunted down and killed and it was an old lion that had probably been kicked out of the pride.

Dangerous night-time lion safari

Small consolation if you are the one eaten, so we decide to stay in our very hot hut all night.

We hear other lion eating stories. We have been accustomed to the well-fed lions of East Africa, but other parts of Africa are different. We arrive at the Skeleton Coast of Namibia too late to see the last of their desert lions. With a few friends, we fly with bush pilots two at a time into a remote camp in the Okavango Delta area of Botswana. The camp is tented but has private toilets. There is no fence around the camp, so it is very open to the surrounding jungle. Canals everywhere, and of course the small dirt landing strip. The bush pilots are very young and daring. For most, this is their first flying job.

At lunch, The Skooter and I meet a doctor and his wife from Kalamazoo, Michigan. Outside of my niece, I have had only one relative, my uncle, who was a doctor, and he was from Kalamazoo. In an amazing twist of fate, this doctor had taken over my uncle's general medical practice.

The doctor tells us a story about a group of his friends who came to a camp like this. After dinner, they all went back to one tent because the men wanted to play cards. Eventually, one of the women said she was tired of sitting around watching the men play cards and was going back to her own tent. She never made it. A lion ate her. I guess the message was, be careful.

That night we have a lovely dinner and then they have a little show for us. I go up the teak stairs ahead of the Skooter. She comes up and sits next to me but seems a little shaken. She says she slipped on the stairs. At the end of the show, I look at her slacks and remark that she must have spilled catsup. Only it isn't catsup; it is blood and lots of it. By that time, everybody has gone to their tents. I am able to get the camp manager but he isn't at all helpful. I ask him what our options are and he says, none until morning when we could fly her to Maun.

Knowing that the rate of AIDS infection in Botswana is running over 50%, I do not want her in a Maun hospital. I tell the manager to go wake up the doctor from Kalamazoo. He says, "I can't do that." and I say, "Oh, yes, you can." Eventually I win out and he does. Since it is now quite late and very dark, he says he will leave the power generator on. He doesn't, and we are in total darkness with only flashlights.

The Kalamazoo doctor couldn't have been better if he had been a reincarnation of my uncle, whom we had loved dearly. He comes to our tent and examines The Skooter's knee. It has been badly cut by her landing on the teak wood stair. He stops the bleeding but says he will have to operate right then and there in the tent. He has all the medical equipment he needs including anaesthetic, internal and external stitches, etc.

It is amazing that he brought all these medical supplies all the way from Kalamazoo. It seems like a miracle to me. My job while the doctor does the surgery from 11:30 p.m. until 2:00 a.m. is to hold the flashlight so he can see. I, too, get a good look at the internal structure of my beloved Skooter's knee, all the while hoping and praying that this would all work out. At one point, the doctor says he has to go back to his tent to get something. Remembering his lion story and fearing that The Skooter had left a trail of blood leading to our tent, I tell him he should not go alone. I go out with him and swing my big flashlight around and try to make noises like a hyena to scare away any inquisitive lion. Actually, a hungry hyena would have been just as bad. There is no night-time guard.

When the doctor leaves at 2:00 a.m., he gives The Skooter some antibiotics to take and says she should stay in bed the next day before trying to travel. He was checking out and moving on, as were our other friends. The next day, The Skooter was feeling her usual lively self. When we began our extensive world traveling to remote places, we had pledged to each other that if we ever had a serious medical problem—either of us—the other would do everything possible to get back quickly to the USA rather than seeking local medical treatment. We had bent our rule, but it all seemed an act of fate, and now it is time to find the best and quickest way home. The Skooter tells me that, while being operated on, she had asked the doctor what his specialty had been and he told her he originally was a brain surgeon before having a stroke. Anyway, I was convinced he did a great job on her knee. After all, I saw it all while holding the flashlight.

Arrangements are made for a bush pilot to fly us to Maun the next day. From there, we take a commercial flight to Johannesburg and then non-stop to Zurich. At Zurich, I make arrangements for a beautiful hotel room with balcony overlooking the lake and downtown Zurich. The Skooter is in a wheelchair and I am tired from pushing it and from the

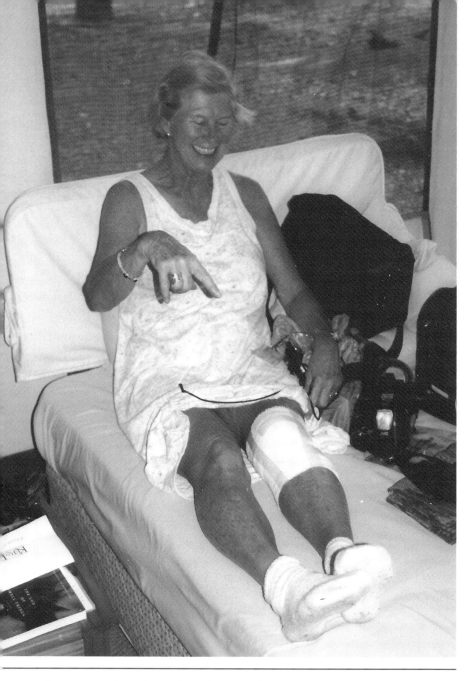

long trip to Zurich. When she says, "Aren't we going to explore downtown Zurich?" I simply say "No, I have made other plans!" We have a
lovely room service dinner on our balcony with a good bottle of red
wine. The next day we fly back to Washington, D. C. A check-up with
our local doctor shows that the doctor from Kalamazoo had done an
excellent job. There is no infection or subsequent problem.

Another time, The Skooter and I decide to visit a remote game park in Rwanda near the border with Uganda where the rumor is that Tutsis are arming and massing for an assault on the Hutus in Rwanda. Later it happens and there is an enormous slaughter, but all is quiet when we are there—too quiet. There is a guard at the gate but we do not see another person in the park all day so it is just The Skooter and I and our guide in our little car.

At the little office by the park entrance there are four very large photos.

1. A man getting out of his vehicle with his camera
2. A lion leaping on him from the rear
3. His wife screaming
4. The lion eating him

Words were not necessary—the message was clear. Do not get out of your vehicle without extreme care, and we didn't, but I have often wondered who took those photos and did they try to save the poor guy?

We roll over the vast terrain both on and off the roads. Some game parks do not allow you to go off road with your vehicle, but our very best experiences were where the driver could follow the animals wherever they went. We did get out of our vehicle for a picnic lunch in a very open spot where we could see in all directions.

Suddenly our driver spots a Cape buffalo that lions have killed and he drives right up to it. Just as suddenly, we are surrounded by lions. The Skooter is delighted as she is taking videos. I count eight lions on all sides of us. A couple of lions are still eating. A few had climbed trees on both sides of us and are lounging on branches. A couple others were at the watering hole on the other side, which must have been the Cape buffalo's destination when they nabbed him. The Cape buffalo is a big, strong animal, so the lions must have done their job with great cooperation.

The Skooter is taking video when a big female lion casually climbed out of her perch in the tree and heads right for her. In somewhat of a panic, the Skooter said "Dave, we've got to get out of here!" I not so reassuringly said "Keep it rolling; it's great video!"

Of course we couldn't have gotten out of there if we had wanted to because we were surrounded on all sides by lions. But they were not hungry lions. Actually the lion heading right for The Skooter wanted to

go to the watering hole and our vehicle just happened to be in the way. The Skooter rolled up her window and watched as the lion sauntered around the vehicle.

We saw many lions over the years but always will remember Rwanda as the best up close and personal. Unfortunately, we heard that the park was destroyed during the war.

Years later, we are in Newport, Rhode Island for a family wedding. The Skooter is in a wheelchair, her ankle patched together with a plate and eleven screws, because she had broken it while training one of our German Shepherds. During an afternoon outing for The Skooter, I am expected to be the tour guide. My back gets worn out getting the wheelchair in and out of the car trunk, so when we come to an antique store, I go in alone. But I had to come back to get her. They had a magnificent, full-size, bronze lion. We fall in love with him. We purchase him and have him shipped to our home where he guards our front door for eleven years before he is promoted to even more important duties, as the Lion Memorial for The Skooter.

Chapter 8

Rhinoceros in the Yemen Souk

The Skooter thinks Yemen will be a great place to visit. We have been on a round-the-world trip with Spencer Welles of National Geographic, tracing the origins of the human genome. His methods include extensive DNA testing indicating that mankind originated in Africa and migrated out through the Middle East, including Yemen, making it one of the oldest centers of civilization.

Yemen is located on the Arabian Peninsula. It is one of the poorest and least developed countries in the Arab world since it lacks much oil. They have many tribal groups and clans but are roughly split 50-50, Sunni-Shiite, while the much larger and richer Kingdom of Saudi

Arabia next door is largely Sunni. All those tribal divisions have historically led to much fighting. Indeed, when we arrive they have just finished a civil war between what had been called North and South Yemen. Now it is called the Republic of Yemen.

Our first stop is in Aden, which used to be a large naval base protecting the British Empire. In Aden it is easy to see who lost the war. There are huge piles of garbage. It is pretty smelly, so we are glad to move on to Sana'a the capital. Sana'a

is very picturesque and obviously they have picked up the garbage. Our first stop is at the University where, though a Harvard connection, we are shown mummies claimed to be as old as any in Egypt. Never have we been so close to such well preserved mummies.

The Skooter wants to get to the souk, which is always a fascinating place in Arab countries. First, a stop at the main hotel, which is our rendezvous spot since we are going alone without a guide. Yemen is such an unstable place, I have not changed any dollars. The official rate is about 6 rials per US dollar. I ask the hotel manager what the market rate is, and he says I can probably get around 32. What a difference! I next ask whether it is legal and he says "Oh yes. In fact, you can even buy with a credit card." Must be difficult to run a hotel, I comment, and he agrees. So we head off to see the town and its fascinating souk, alone, at our own leisurely pace.

The old clay and brick buildings of Sana'a are architecturally well-preserved and beautiful, with hand-carved, wooden doors and old bronze handles in some cases. Everything is a shade of brown. The peo-

ple are most interesting of all. The men all carry curved daggers, which look quite lethal, around their waists. Everywhere we see men walking in twosomes with their robes and daggers, holding hands. Everybody is also chewing, but it isn't tobacco; it is *khat*, which is all around in green piles on the ground, freely and openly sold. We are told that *khat* is a mild narcotic that they chew all day. *Khat* is supposedly far and away the biggest cash crop in all of Yemen.

The Skooter and I are both fascinated by the hustle and bustle of the souk. People and stalls are everywhere; narrow alleys lead in all directions. Our first business is to get some local money—but not too much because it will probably be impossible to change back into dollars. Sure enough, I negotiate a deal using my Visa card and get over 30 rials per dollar. I split it with The Skooter so we can each pursue our own shopping interests, hopefully without getting separated in the crowded alleys.

In the Arab world of a souk, there is no fixed price; everything is negotiated. The seller sizes you up and you size him up. He knows you are a tourist and, he hopes, a dumb tourist. The item he is selling may be real or a cheap knock-off. He knows; you don't. Sound like he has an advantage? He does.

How do you try to overcome this advantage? First start absurdly low. If he asks the equivalent of ten dollars, offer one dollar. He will

laugh, so you laugh too. After all, you want this to be a friendly negotiation. Time is on his side. Arab merchants are patient and are used to haggling endlessly. Americans tend to be impatient and Arabs know it. You must act as uninterested in buying the item as you can. He will be trying to size up your real interest. There is nothing wrong with saying, "That is my best price" and then starting to leave. If he lets you leave, maybe it is a decent price and you can always come back. If he tries to stop you, you continue to haggle. The same principles apply in business and, believe me, Americans are mostly inferior negotiators.

The Skooter lets me negotiate for her, but she makes it all too obvious when she really wants something, and then gets upset with me when I can't close the deal. Anyway, we each buy a few treasures and then continue to explore the souk. It is very complex, but the Arabs all seem to be scurrying somewhere in an organized manner.

My curiosity leads me to discover how they manufacture all those curved daggers the men wear around their waists. It is very organized and specialized. One shop makes and sharpens blades only. Then the blades are taken to another shop which makes and assembles handles. The next shop makes and assembles the final product, complete with holster and leather belt. The shops are not adjacent or even in the same area, so there is much transporting back and forth.

Suddenly we realize that it has gotten dark, but there are lights and all the activity continues. Then all of a sudden there is total darkness. The power has gone off everywhere. We are standing there startled and dumbfounded. The Arabs scurry to close their shops and protect their inventory, as if they know the power is not coming back on. We have no idea which way to go to get out of the souk and there is no one to ask. So we are standing there in the dark with the people all gone and no idea what to do.

But The Skooter is unfazed. It will all work out, it always has, she reassures me. It is so dark and deserted that we look in all directions for some clue on how to make a move. And there it is: a faint light in the distance. Maybe it is the Star of Bethlehem. I quip. Whatever. We follow the distant light to its source; it is a lighted shop. We are delighted and relieved. It is a shop selling antiquities; there are a couple of Americans there from museums buying. The shop has its own generator.

The museum buyers tell us this is one of the best places in the world to buy antiquities. People are desperate for hard currency—real money—in order to survive. There are so many authentic old items I would like to own that I have a hard time deciding. Yemen was long ago a center for Jewish goldsmiths, so they are concentrating on those items. Finally I decide on an ancient shield made from rhinoceros hide, with bronze ornamentation. The museum people assure me that it is authentic; centuries ago they did have wild animals like tigers, lions, and rhinos roaming these lands.

The Skooter and I thank everybody. We ask for directions on which way to go to leave the souk and where we might find a taxi. It isn't easy in the total darkness, but miraculously we do get out and eventually find a taxi. The driver has obviously been chewing *khat* all day and is very high, singing away in Arabic, with the car radio on high. We think of changing taxis but there are no others. I try to explain where we want to go—the hotel—but he doesn't speak or understand English. I write it out for him but I don't think he can read either. I have another problem—I am out of local currency. I tell him I have to pay him in US dollars. He looks at it but doesn't know what it is.

The big questions are: is he capable of driving, does he know where he is going, and will he go? He is singing and happy, and off he goes. The combination of *khat* and Arabic music is a good one and we get to the hotel. I pay him in dollars but I think I could have paid him in any worthless currency. The Skooter and I are ready for a nightcap as our friends welcome us back, fearing that we had been kidnapped.

Chapter 9

Independence Day

Independence Day is a big deal all over the world, not just in the U.S. The Skooter and I were fortunate enough to celebrate a few, not because we planned it that way, but purely by happenstance. One gave us not only great happiness but also a feeling of a bright future; the other a sense of foreboding and explosiveness, of some sort of disaster waiting to happen.

We always loved celebrating the 4th of July anywhere. It seemed to give our country great cohesiveness and joy. It is a family event with lots of small children participating. We just assumed it had been that way since 1776 and would always be that way in the future. Fireworks were always a big part of the celebration, but not guns.

So when we happened to be in Oslo, Norway on their Independence Day we anticipated more of the same and we were not disappointed, actually thrilled and excited by what we saw and participated in. Norway became independent from Sweden by referendum in 1905. The Kingdom of Norway is a constitutional monarchy, today with about 5 million people in all, about 1 million of whom live in Oslo. Norway has extensive social networks and stresses integration of ethnic minorities.

Norway was a key part of the old Hanseatic League. Its climate is harsh and its people hardy; a heritage of Vikings who knew the sea and trading. Unfortunately Norway's independence was interrupted by a German Nazi invasion in World War II. So they really appreciate their independence. Sweden cooperated and did not get invaded.

Anyway, the celebration begins with a huge parade down the main avenue to the King's Palace. The participation is really impressive, with families large and small, with big and little kids in tow. Everybody seems happy, waving flags. The happiest of all seem to be the graduating high school seniors who are scurrying about in either red or blue jump suits signifying whether they go to the commercial or technical school. They surround some rather large motorized wagons loaded with kegs of cold beer.

Norwegians have a history of being hardy drinkers of hard spirits. That, combined with narrow roads and mountains led to a high auto accident rate. The country has also been blessed with huge deposits of oil, mostly offshore, which were developed very efficiently. This all led to the fourth highest per capita income in the world. To solve the resulting drunk driving problem, Norway passed some of the world's toughest laws against drinking and driving. Essentially if you do it, you go to jail. So Norway responded with non-drinking, "designated drivers" and it has worked.

At the parade in Oslo, the graduating high school seniors in their blue or red jump suits have their own designated beer wagons, driven, of course, by non-drinking, "designated drivers". After the parade, unlimited beer drinking begins and lasts all afternoon; a good time was had by all. The younger kids went home with mom and dad. It is a lively scene but no one is offensive. It is all over on the streets of Oslo by dark; another Independence Day is history.

Then there was Karachi in Pakistan, a big city with almost as many people as all of Norway. Karachi is a seaport and former capital. Muslim yes, but with many racial and ethnic divides. The Skooter and I have always liked visiting Muslim cities because they were colorful and active.

Pakistan had achieved independence from the British in 1947 through the Indian Independence of Act which partitioned India into the Dominion of India and the Dominion of Pakistan. Pakistan later changed its name to The Islamic Republic of Pakistan. At first an East and West Pakistan were created, but the East changed its name to Bangladesh. The British were anxious to get out and many Muslim refugees were driven from their homes. India was firmly under Hindu control. Pakistan was firmly under Muslim control. Control of the Kashmir region in the north between them never was established. Pakistan hated India and Hindus. The Skooter loved them all and thought they should at least respect each other.

The ceremonies in Karachi feature lots of waving of green and white flags, and speeches, but not much of a family atmosphere. The Skooter and I decide to explore downtown Karachi on our own. There is much hustle and bustle, and it is very colorful. The buses and trucks are elaborately painted in very bright colors, not just for the holiday but also for regular use. People are going in all directions and there is no indication that this is a special day. While Pakistan is certainly all Muslim, it has not created a very cohesive society. There is a certain tension in the air, highlighted by the number of men running around with live ammunition belts hung over their shoulders. Strange! Where there is lots of ammunition, there must be guns, right?

So we explore and, sure enough, there are lots of guns not so hidden behind counters in shops and elsewhere. We haven't seen or heard fireworks but decide we would have trouble telling fireworks from gunshots, so we decide to retreat to safer quarters.

Chapter 10

Real Dragons Still Exist in the Wild

The Skooter says we have to go to Indonesia

to see the animals and temples. I say where in Indonesia? Indonesia is made up of 17,508 islands with over 200,000,000 people who have probably driven out most of the animals in order to survive. Indonesia has been independent since World War II.

We do see lots of temples in this fascinating country, which has been an important trading post since the 7th century and has survived centuries of Dutch colonialism. In terms of ethnic diversity, it is hard to

beat Indonesia. It has hundreds of native ethnic and linguistic groups, although it is considered nominally Muslim.

We do get to Sumatra and see the territory of the mighty Sumatran Tiger. Alas, there are none left. But there is one unique animal left in Indonesia that even has its very own island. Komodo Island is home to the Komodo dragon, a very unique animal that, until 1911, was thought to be mythological. Komodo dragons weigh up to 255 pounds, are as long as 10 feet, and are carnivorous, living off deer, water buffalo, wild boar, and an occasional human being. They move quickly (18 mph) over short distances.

The Komodo dragon has incredibly sharp teeth and a venomous bite that secretes up to 80 specific bacteria and an anti-coagulant so its victims keep bleeding. They can swim; they hunt and ambush their prey. They are protected by Indonesian law in Komodo National Park. They virtually own Komodo Island. An awesome animal!

The only approach to Komodo Island is by boat. There is no dock, so it's a wet landing—wading ashore. At least there are no dragons on the beach when we arrive. The Komodo dragons freely roam the island so we have to be on alert. We have a guide, and our hiking destination is the ranger station, so we are off on the path always looking for dragons lurking somewhere. The hike is uneventful and the terrain not difficult. Our guide does point out the spot where a tired tourist sat down, fell asleep, and was eaten by a Komodo dragon.

The rangers show us a variety of Komodo dragons up close and personal for picture taking, etc. Fortunately they are well caged. They also do a feeding demo with a goat, so we have no doubt about the sharpness of the teeth or their quickness. Then we do the hike back to shore and re-board the boat. The Skooter is happy that she has viewed and photographed still another unique animal.

Chapter 11

The KGB Tries to Recruit The Skooter

Gorbachev is now in control and big changes are taking place in the Soviet Union—or are they really? Through Yale, The Skooter and I have an opportunity to go to Moscow, Kiev, and St. Petersburg with two professors and a small group. At this time, I am a top executive in charge of various commercial operations for my company. However, the really big business is aerospace, including some of the country's biggest intercontinental ballistic missiles. As a result, I do sit in on various CIA briefings on the mighty Soviet Union from time to time. None of our top executives has been to the Soviet Union, so I will be a first. I rate a special individual CIA briefing. Essentially they tell me to watch my step: the Soviets will not believe that I have nothing to do with nuclear ballistic missiles. Good advice.

We fly by Finnair from Helsinki to Moscow, arriving at night. The terminal is dark and dreary. The agent takes my passport at a large desk and keeps staring at me. Then he looks down, then back at me, then behind his desk again as if checking his computer. This goes on so long that I do something I know I should not do. I take a peek behind the desk to see what he has there. Nothing! No computer—not even a pad and pencil. Strictly an attempt at intimidation!

We go on to the hotel, which is one of the strangest we have ever seen. It is huge, but built in distinct compartments. It is winter and very cold outside, but in this hotel you have to go outside and back in another entrance to get to a restaurant. We seem to have a very special room because there is a desk and a big Russian woman seated there, right outside our door. I call her the house-mother, there to watch over us. I feel sure the room is bugged, and tell The Skooter to watch what she says.

Our tour of The Kremlin and Red Square is fascinating. So much history to absorb! We buy a colorful watercolor painting from an artist on Red Square, all the more interesting because most of the buildings are so drab. We go to Gum's Department Store; it is a shock—nothing that you would really want to buy. Even more shocking is there are no cash registers; they are using the abacus everywhere.

We have lots of time to wander alone. I do not think we are being followed, but I am sure our room is regularly searched, since I set little traps for them. We walk the streets and stop in various shops. Everywhere the abacus. In fact, in the whole trip we do not see a cash register or a computer. The people we do see on the streets look very glum and will not look you in the eye. No one talks to anyone else. Of course, we go to see a well-preserved Lenin and he is about as talkative as the others. We are told that the young people like to go to the monuments to get married. The stores are full of goods that no one wants to buy. The plant managers get paid for what they produce, not what sells. I remember one store that had shelves filled with canned prunes. The cans had been there so long that they were rusting.

The ballet and other artistic performances we see are excellent. The streets seem clean and safe—and we see why. Gorbachev is trying to crack down on vodka sales; the Russians do love their vodka. We do see a drunk, but he is quickly whisked off the streets in the strong arms of the police.

In all, Moscow seems a rather cold, unfriendly, drab place, with everybody suspicious of everybody else, so we are happy to leave for the airport. On getting there, we are told our flight has been canceled. There are hundreds of people waiting, many sitting or lying on the floor. There appears to be a large delegation of Cubans. Not to worry, we are told. We are considered a special cultural delegation so they will "bump" Russians off another flight so we can get to Kiev.

The Aeroflot flight to Kiev is one of the strangest we have ever been on. The plane and the seats are old and rickety. We are seated amongst Russians and no one speaks a word to anyone, not even the Russians. The unspoken message is "conform or you are in trouble". On arrival in Kiev, we taxi to the terminal and stop. The door is opened and I start to get up to get my coat. Wrong! I get fierce stares from all the Russians and slump back in my seat. Suddenly the pilots and stewardesses all come marching down the aisle—no band—and get off the plane first. Then the passengers can get up and struggle off.

At first glance. Kiev looks very much like Moscow, but on closer inspection it does seem a little more European. There are some flower pots in the windows of some flats—none in Moscow. There are a few entrepreneurs trying to sell something on the streets. Even a few flowers for sale. We get to our hotel; it is a Soviet relic. Old and no charm! Our room has steam heat. You cannot turn it off if you wanted to. There is some toilet paper, but no soap and no shower curtain. We go to a forgettable dinner. When we return to our room, there is no toilet paper. We conclude that the maid is stealing it. That night, it starts to snow, and snow, and snow. Over 20 inches; we are snowed in. Then an amazing thing happens in the morning. All the workers come out of the offices with snow shovels and start to shovel the snow by hand into dump trucks. The communist system at work!

Our next stop is St. Petersburg, where the Russians did a fantastic job of restoration and preserving old treasures from the days of the Czars. The Hermitage is one of the best museums in the world, loaded with treasures. It is not very well organized and huge in size, so you could spend days exploring it. Of course the palaces have been meticulously rebuilt. They are gorgeous buildings with grounds maintained in splendid fashion. Leningrad suffered greatly in World War II. It was never captured by the Germans but it was blockaded and shelled without mercy. Even though the city was largely destroyed, the Russians managed to hide and save contents of the palaces and then meticulously rebuild them with the skilled artisans available. I am particularly intrigued by the gorgeous amber room they had built. The original amber room was dismantled and hidden but was never found after the war.

We have good Intourist Russian guides on the trip, very helpful and friendly, but the system is strange. In each city, we have a different guide. The guides tell us they are never allowed to actually meet their counterpart, even at point of transfer, so none of the guides know each other. Security!

Our hotel in what is now called Saint Petersburg is elegant by Russian standards. It had been built by the Swedes, we are told. Our room is

Summer Palace, St. Petersburg

still searched regularly. There are lots of Scandinavian tourists. Vodka is cheap for a big week-end. The food is still bad except for the ice cream.

Having seen most if not all of the major historic sites, we finally get some time to ourselves. The Skooter and I decide to explore the city on our own: lots of walking and people watching. Suddenly, out of nowhere, a young man comes up to us speaking perfect English. For the whole trip so far, no Russian has been friendly, except maybe our guides. The hotel bartender laughed at me when I asked for ice with my straight vodka. Most people did not even want to look at us.

Now this guy is saying he is a florist and likes Americans and wants to be friends. He wants us to come to a coffee shop for tea, or better yet ice cream. Then he says we should come to his flat to see his antique samovar.

It all sounds so unreal that I am stunned, but The Skooter is delighted to be talking with what she thinks is a real Russian. She keeps the conversation going and even writes down the guy's name and address because he wants her to send him postcards. Finally after turning down all his overtures, I ask him to point the way to a taxi stand as it is dark and we have to get back to the group at the hotel. He does and we take off, but when we get to the taxi stand, there he is. He says the taxi stand is very busy and he will have his driver take us to the hotel. Another couple from our group shows up giving us some courage and we agree. His driver is in a red army uniform and an open Jeep. We take off with The Skooter in the front seat with the driver and three of us in the back. The Skooter, always trying to be friendly, asks the driver if he speaks English. His answer is a simple "NO."

It is quite obvious that our friendly florist is really KGB, so we are very happy to get back to the hotel and rejoin our group. Our guide says it was a good thing we did not go to his flat because then we could have been arrested for contacting a dissident and the guides could not have done anything for us.

We have our farewell dinner and are glad to be rid of the florist. But wait! The next morning he is back. I refuse to talk with him, but The Skooter does, under my watchful eye. He gives her a bunch of posters, which we don't even look at but she packs. On the way to the airport I ask to read The Skooter's diary and tell her it is boring—mostly about what we ate and drank.

At the airport, we are in a check-out line and it is strange. The guard is looking through our friend's medicine bag and stealing just about everything. For example, she picks up a bottle of aspirin and asks what it is and what it is for. My friend says it is for headaches. The guard says she has a headache as she slips it in her pocket. And so it goes, item after item.

Finally, it is our turn but we are abruptly pulled out of line and taken to a special area for thorough searching and questioning. Surprisingly, the guards concentrate on The Skooter, not me. They go over everything she has, meticulously. They come across her diary, of course, and get all agitated. They find the florist's address and now seem convinced there is some sinister plot; they call their supervisor. The supervisor calls his superior. The Skooter is shaken—a rare occurrence—but the grilling has been intense. Their questioning proceeds with a strong element of intimidation. I want to tell them that the florist is really KGB, but I can't say a word. Finally a big Russian arrives and says to let us go.

As quickly as we can, we rush to get on our Finnair flight but we must march methodically. Soldiers are all around, including two standing at attention with rifles at the bottom of the stairway. When the plane finally heads down the runway, everybody claps and cheers—happy to be leaving the "evil empire" I guess.

Helsinki is a total contrast. Bright and cheerful. People smiling and rushing about. It is Christmas season. There are no decorations in Russia. We are so happy to be in Finland it is hard to describe. Gorbachev may be in charge nominally, but our feeling is that the KGB still controls Russia. In fact, while we did not know it at the time, there was an agent named Putkin in Saint Petersburg while we were there. I will never know why, but for some reason, the CIA never debriefed me on our return. If they had, I would have told them what a mess the civilian economy is: no computers, a lack of toilet paper and plenty of unsmiling, unhappy, fearful people.

Chapter 12

The Skeleton Coast and Namibia

The Skooter has read about a place that is remote and intriguing. Years before we had been to Portugal and visited the spot in its furthest west from which Vasco da Gama would plan his explorations. Da Gama was focused on finding a route by ship around Africa to develop the spice trade with the Far East. He planned the voyages meticulously, but he never personally went on any of them. That way, if the explorers did not return, Da Gama could just send out another until, finally, success was achieved.

It was a dangerous trip down the west coast of Africa. Strong storms come up from the Antarctic across a vast expanse of cold open water. Warm air on dry winds from Africa cross the Namib Desert and meet the cold sea and the Benguela current, causing impenetrable fog. The result, over the centuries, were many shipwrecks, earning this area

the name Skeleton Coast. Once a ship had fallen prey to a storm, the fog, or currents, the surviving sailors' problems had just begun as the coasts are but a thin barren line between the pounding ocean and the stark desert interior where oases are very rare. The area is also called the Coast of Skulls.

Namibia itself has a very interesting history. The Germans first settled Luderitz in the far southern part of the country. We fly to the capital, Windhoek, and get a car and driver to head for Luderitz. Windhoek turns out to be a pleasant town but it is a shock to hear everyone speaking German. Namibia was a German colony until 1915 and was called German Southwest Africa. It was invaded in World War I by South African and British forces. At the end of the war, South Africa received a League of Nations mandate to administer the territory. That mandate was revoked by the UN in 1978, but South Africa continued to hang on for another ten years. Namibia finally achieved its independence in 1990.

Namibia's economy is supported by diamonds. When in Windhoek, I visit DeBeers' offices but I am rudely rejected as a tourist. The countryside heading south is semi-arid, with some farmers trying to hang on by cattle ranching. As we near Luderitz, there are huge chain-link fences on both sides of the highway. Signs on the fences proclaim no trespassing—at the risk of being shot. Also, there are snowplows along the road, not for snow, but to remove the huge drifts of sand blown by the fierce winds. The drifts have to be plowed constantly to keep the road open. Protecting the diamond mines is obviously serious business.

Luderitz is a very small town but shows its German influence. I find a small rock on the beach that I think might be a raw diamond, but after intensive testing (scratching glass), I decide it is just quartz. Diamond is the hardest mineral known and will scratch anything. There is no sign that Luderitz is a diamond-mining center and we head north, past what is still a South African naval base at Walvis Bay. We reach Swakopmund.

Swakopmund is a delightful little town that makes you feel you are in Germany. It is located right on the ocean, so we enjoy some great fresh seafood: the local lobster tails, grilled. Then we are ready to move on to our great Skeleton Coast adventure. We take off in a very small plane and head north. Surprisingly, the landing is on a sandy beach.

We are met by a Jeep and driven north through the debris of numerous shipwrecks and come upon a large live bird entangled in a fishing net on the beach. Naturally, we have to rescue the bird, now identified as a Cameron. Foolishly, I try to help our guide untangle the bird; the panicked and ungrateful guy takes a bite out of my finger. The Skooter has little sympathy and tells me to go soak it in the ocean. Easier said than done with the surf. The bird flies free and, I hope, grateful.

We arrive at our remote camp in a small oasis away from the ocean. First order of business is to stop the bleeding and bandage my finger. The camp is very primitive. We have a small tent with two cots, a long ways from any toilet facilities; thus a bucket between the cots. Wild animals need water so it seems likely we will have visitors at night. Neither The Skooter nor I intend to venture out of the tent. But something else happens, entirely unexpectedly, at night. It is very warm, but a strong wind and rainstorm come out of the East from central Africa. Our tent is almost blown away and begins leaking badly. Everything gets wet. But eventually, without our getting much sleep, morning comes and it is sunny again.

The next days are days of exploration. Our little camp is surrounded by sights to see. The most spectacular are the enormous sand dunes, called the "singing dunes" because of the weird noises the wind makes as it howls through the dunes. Like little kids, we slide down the biggest dune on our fannies while listening to the singing sound. We visit an abandoned amethyst mine. We visit two seal colonies—one a noisy breeding colony, the other quieter where the guide says none of them breed.

There are a few elephants around but not too many. The guides say it is hard for them to survive the harsh climate and dry desert conditions. The last desert lion died the year before. The temperature swings are enormous depending on whether the wind is coming off a cold South Atlantic Ocean from the west, or from the east out of the interior of Africa.

The last night our explorations are mostly along the ocean and we are told we will camp on the beach. This campsite, however, is entirely different. Instead of conventional tents, there are small wooden tepee structures. We are told that regular tents would just blow away in the fierce winds. After a beach barbecue we adjourn early to our small humble wooden hideaway. All night the wind roars, shaking but not destroying our shelter. It is difficult to sleep with the strange noises and cold but once again the sun comes up for some striking views.

Our wooden tent

To the north is Angola where they are engaged in a civil war no one seems able to win. We are taken to a native village and told that the natives in Namibia are quite peaceful because the Germans ruthlessly wiped out any belligerent trouble-makers. The Skooter and I board a small plane—I in the co-pilot's seat—even though I do not have the slightest idea how to fly. Unshaven for days I now look like I belong in Africa. The bandage on my finger has not been changed and is a very dirty brown color blending in with the sand dunes. I am convinced the finger must be infected after this lack of care. The landing strip looks to us like they neglected to remove a lot of stones but our bush pilot manoeuvres around them to get us airborne, only to be confronted by what looks like a tornado. I figure he will fly around it but no, he heads right into it.

We survive the shaking little plane and land at our goal, Etosha National Park, although the pilot doesn't seem to know which little strip he should land on. Etosha is built around a dried up lakebed that looks like an endless pan of silvery white sand. When the rains come there is water and thus lots of wild animals to view and photograph. I am pleased to shower and shave and take the bandage off my wounded finger, which looks shriveled up and dead but is not infected.

Namibia has many game parks, including private ones, which we visit. At one, the owner has his own plane so he can go up and find where the big animals are and direct his drivers on land by radio where to go. Eventually it is back to Windhoek and on to more adventure.

Chapter 13

Syria

The Skooter says we have a chance to go to Syria and we must go. I try to give my usual weak resistance by pointing out what a bad neighborhood they are in, surrounded by Iraq, Jordan, Iran, Turkey, Lebanon and Israel with whom they are always fighting wars. Besides their leader is a ruthless dictator named Hafez al-Assad who slaughters his own people at the least provocation, ala the 1982 Hama massacre. The Skooter counters that Syria encompasses some of the most interesting parts of the ancient world: one of the oldest, continuously occupied, large cities in the world, Damascus; the route of ancient migrations from Africa; the Phoenician civilization that controlled the Mediterranean; the invasion of the Crusaders from Europe; and all the history of the Euphrates River. Besides. things are calm now.

The Skooter wins as usual, and we are off. Modern Syria was formed as a French mandate after World War I. It has fertile plains, des-

Billboard of Hafez al-Assad

Skooter at Mosque   *Damascus*

erts, mountains, and a Mediterranean seashore. It has many diverse ethnic and religious groups of people, including Alawites, Shia, Kurds, Christians, Assyrians, Druze, Turks, Armenians, and Sunni Arabs, who are by far the largest at about 50 to 60%. Assad was part of a Ba'athist Party take-over in 1966 when Syria gained its independence. Assad controlled the military and took over as dictator in 1970. The Ba'athist Party was an Alawite group that gained power, although they represented only about 11% of the population. Assad and the Ba'athists used hatred of Israel to help unite Syria. In June of 1967, Syria fought a war with Israel and lost. In October, 1973, Syria fought another war with Israel called the Yom Kippur War, and lost. Syria had tried a union with Egypt starting in 1958 but that was broken up. Egypt made peace with Israel but not Syria. In 1976, Syria began a 30-year occupation of neighboring Lebanon. In 1981, Israel annexed the Golan Heights overlooking Damascus.

Syria is a relatively small country. The Skooter and I intended to see it all, starting with ancient Damascus. Damascus was well worth exploring on our own. The Skooter found an old goldsmith who had made a beautiful 24-karat gold bracelet and she wanted it. One problem: he did not know what a credit card was and would not accept US dollars. Not to worry; The Skooter found a way to get Syrian

Crusader castle

money. Surprisingly, the next big shopping stop was a Jewish merchant selling wonderful silk, and she had to buy. When we got home it was made into a fabulous evening gown, my very favorite of hers.

Having been to many cities where armed police and soldiers are very much in evidence, it surprises us that they are not in Damascus. Everything seems quite open, but the people are a little suspicious of strangers. The old buildings look old and not in the best repair. The souk is interesting but not on a par with others in the Arab world. From what little contact we do have with the people, it is obvious that fear of Israel has been firmly ingrained. The Israelis are encamped on the Golan Heights overlooking Damascus, according to what the people are told. Statues and full-sized, huge billboards of Assad are everywhere, as are plain-clothed security operatives.

Soon we head north and west through Homs where so many were slaughtered, and the Crusader country where we visit a marvelous well-preserved castle. The number of very blonde little kids attests to the Crusader heritage. We go through some pretty mountains where there is skiing. Then to Latakia on the seashore, which had been the heart of the Phoenician civilization. The Phoenicians were great sailors and controlled the Mediterranean for a long period. We had

been fortunate to spend some time in Tunisia where the Phoenicians had built a fantastic sea base that is well-preserved. Tunisia was a big part of the North African granary that fed the mighty Roman Empire so Roman ruins abound in many regions.

We head to Palmyra which was built by the Aramean Kingdom in the 4th century BC. The ruins are remarkably well-preserved and you can really get the feeling you are living in that ancient city. From there we head to Aleppo where we stay overnight and thoroughly explore on our own. The souk is smaller but better than the one in Damascus. After a long day of exploration we are ready to head for our hotel to relax so we get a taxi and have the usual language problems. We think we get it understood where we want to go and the driver takes off. It soon becomes apparent to me that we are heading in the opposite direction of the hotel and the driver is smiling and happy. I tell The Skooter that I think we are being kidnapped. She says not to worry it will be all right. We are in a very nice section of town and soon the driver is pointing out pretty houses and other landmarks to us. It finally becomes apparent to us that the driver is very proud of Aleppo and giving us a free tour of its better parts.

We head back to Damascus for one last stop, the residence of the U.S. Ambassador. Over cocktails and dinner we have a delightful evening of conversation with him. He takes the approach that, now that we have been all over Syria, what have we learned, rightly or wrongly. It is very apparent that Assad has used hatred of Israel and almost continuous war to hold his ethnically and religiously diverse country together. After all he is an Alawite who make up only 11% of the population.

Even as we enjoy our travels, we are aware that Assad has one of the worst human rights records in the world. He relies on credit from Russia and Iran. The economy is very regulated. Syria has very little oil. Assad's scare tactic to his people, about the Israelis on the Golan Heights ready at any time to swoop down on Damascus, is totally false. The Golan Heights is occupied by a contingent of U.N. troops. The one hope held out is that Assad will not live forever. Even if he manages to install his son,

Bashar as his successor, Bashar was educated in the U.S. and, hopefully, will be better. We all know how that turned out: like father like son.

Chapter 14

Gross National Happiness in Bhutan

After visiting so many war zones and potential war zones, I ask The Skooter if we can't just go some place where it is peaceful and the people are happy. She says she has just the right place: The Kingdom of Bhutan in the Himalayas, between India, which she loved, and Nepal, which we had already visited. Only one problem, they don't want tourists.

I investigate and she is right on all counts. Also, Bhutan is not easy to get to. Air Bhutan has only two little planes and one airport, Paro. We learn intriguing things. For example, there are no lawyers. Parties are expected to settle disputes between themselves. Also there is only one traffic light in the whole country. It's in the capital, Thimphu. The country is very environmentally friendly; you need a permit to cut down a tree.

The government's main policy for its people and growth is Gross National Happiness, not developing Gross National Product.

The Skooter finds a couple to go with us; I am charged with finding the way to do it. That way was to hire a good, well-connected travel agency in Bhutan and make all ar-

rangements through them. Arrangements are made so we can go during The Festival of Paro, a giant celebration in this small Buddhist country. We have to fly through Bangladesh to get to Paro, an airport that, at the time, had no equipment for instrument landings. I get a chance to ask the pilot how he does it. He says they turn toward Mount Everest and head on in. I never got a chance to ask my second question which was going to be, what do you do if it is foggy?

As soon as we get off the plane, we know we are going to like the place. The colors are bright, the people smiling and friendly, the greetings seem sincere. Our hotel is humble but clean (they have since built a fancy new hotel in Paro). We find the first big event is going to be a pre-dawn visit to the opening of the festival. Why so early? They have a huge ancient tapestry that is stored and only comes out once a year. It is hung briefly at the center of the festival venue, and then is rolled up and put away before sunrise so that the bright sun cannot cause it to fade. The festival is a big Buddhist event and we are right in the middle of it. It is also very much a family event with everyone all dressed up in their very finest, even the kids. The Bhutanese are supposed to wear traditional dress and they produce beautiful, colorful fabrics, so all in all, it is a fantastic scene.

The people and kids are all friendly. The little kids proudly show us their simple plastic toys, which I presume they have received as some sort of holiday gift. None of the kids do any begging, as you see in so many other poor or Third World countries. We are accepted and move along in line with the others. We do not know the language so we can only smile. I am not sure how appropriate that is in some sort of religious ceremony with incense. Anyway, we get what I think is some sort of blessing from the Buddhist priests. All is well.

We thoroughly cover both the Paro Festival and Paro itself. Archery is the national sport in Bhutan; they are good at what seem to be enormous distances. (They tell us that the best bows and arrows are made in Salt Lake City, USA.) The Crown Prince comes to visit the festivities, seemingly alone as he mingles with the people—certainly there are no apparent secret service agents or bodyguards. We visit the local Buddhist monastery and eat the local food.

We head out of Paro by car. The roads are narrow and made out of crushed stone. What is unusual is that the stone is crushed by hand: people squat and break bigger pieces into smaller with hand-held hammers. At least that must provide a lot of government jobs!

One of our first stops is the famous "Tigers Nest" perched high in the mountains on the edge of a cliff. There, the Buddha apparently meditated in a cave for 3 months. The Skooter and I are determined to make the trek up the steep trail. For her it is easy, for me it is a "killer". But I never realized that going back down would be even more difficult. I buy an antique Buddhist burial bell just in case, but I finally make it and silently vow that that will be my very last mountain trek! My knees have given out.

On to Thimphu, the capital. We see the one traffic light in Bhutan on the main square where our humble hotel is located. The town is small

enough to walk around but we are driven to the highlights. At a museum, I buy an antique carrying case for a small Buddha. We visit several training centers where young people are learning to make the local crafts and artwork.

The evening turns out to be a particular delight. We are taken to

The Tiger's Nest

a small dinner at the local golfing country club. There are 11 holes for golf; I guess that always keeps your score low. There are several government ministers at the dinner and they are all young—I would guess in their thirties— and all educated in the US in places like the University of Kansas. College basketball's "March Madness" is taking place and they are very interested in talking about it. Currently there is no TV or Internet in Bhutan but it is coming. The ban was lifted in 1999. We have a good conversation with the Minister of Telecommunications. He is young and sharp. Will TV and the Internet contribute to gross national happiness? They think it will. There are also a few business people involved in exports at the dinner. It appears Bhutan is opening up to tourists and more modern ways. In fact, Bhutan changes from an absolute monarchy to a constitutional government run by a council of ministers and elected national assembly in 2008.

We head back to Paro and our departure pondering whether this little country, where you still need a permit to cut down a tree, can modernize and still maintain its gross national happiness goal. We stop at many little villages. The construction of almost everything is wood and white-washed stucco. The people like to paint decorations on their houses; the bright colors stand out against the stark whiteness. One of the favorites is a big graphic, realistic painting of a penis over the front door. The Skooter is embarrassed and we have no explanation of what it is supposed to mean. I jokingly tell her it, sex, is an important aspect of gross national happiness. The people of Bhutan do seem happy and are consistently rated the happiest in Asia. It is a welcome contrast to some of our other trips, so we are very much in favor of gross national happiness as a national goal.

We later learn that the one traffic light in the country is being removed.

Chapter 15

Thatcher, Oxford, and NATO

It is 1980. Margaret Thatcher has been elected British Prime Minister, the first woman to hold that honor. The British economy is in ongoing recession and there is a "winter of discontent" in England. I have an opportunity to go with a small group of businessmen to Oxford to learn what Thatcher intends to do about it all through her newly appointed ministers.

I am excited about the trip since it also includes a side-trip to Brussels for a full day's briefing from all of NATO's top ministers. I come home to tell The Skooter about my plans. She says she wants to go. I say you can't; this is a group of men.

I take off with the group. We get to Oxford and check in at university facilities that will be home base for the next 3 days. I get a telephone call from The Skooter; she says she is coming and knows how to get to Oxford on her own and will room with me if I just tell her where I am, which I do. The Skooter is intent on traveling and even though this is not an exotic location, it sounds exciting and she doesn't want to miss it. I find the General who is in charge of our group to explain to him that my wife is joining me and hope that he is understanding. As it turns out, he is. Actually his wife has come with him, so now we have two women in our little group.

The briefings go on in historic Oxford but also London. The atmosphere seems somber as the ministers stress how uncompetitive England is in every industry. My standard question gets to be this: if you are uncompetitive in all these industries and want to get out of them, where are the jobs going to come from? Everyone can't be a financial worker and live in London. There doesn't seem to be a well thought-out program, but maybe they are stressing the negative on purpose since they expect serious labor opposition based on the platform they ran on to enact more privatization, reduce the power of labor unions, and deregulate—particularly the financial industry. We do not hear from Thatcher directly but we are treated like royalty on the food and beverage side.

We leave England feeling that Margaret Thatcher faces a very difficult situation, but we do not understand the tenacity of The Iron Lady. History proves she is a very remarkable leader and very successful in ways that are largely unanticipated.

On to Brussels and NATO. The headquarters are quite sumptuous and we await our high-level briefing. The morning briefings are good but there is a certain tension in the air. Actually everyone seems to be anticipating lunch and soon we find out why. At 11:30 a.m., lunch starts, with fancy canapés and cocktails, then so many courses I can't count them all. Of course, lots of good red or white wine. Finally, a delicious desert. But wait, that is not the end. We adjourn from the table and everyone is served after-dinner drinks, even though this is a luncheon. And large Cuban cigars for the men. The Skooter and the General's wife are the only women in attendance. Then at 2:30 p.m., it is back to the briefing room. A three-hour luncheon extravaganza!

The afternoon starts out on a high note, with a Norwegian who is in charge of naval activities discussing NATO naval capabilities. Next comes a Greek minister who discusses procurement. He has slides to present and proceeds to turn out all the lights. It is soon very quiet except for muffled sounds of snoring. Everyone including the General, our leader, and his wife has gone to sleep. I fight it but I cannot resist even though I feel very sorry for the speaker. The Skooter is out cold like the others. I cannot remember if the seminar ever regained any momentum but The Skooter and I, who know Brussels well, are all too glad to skip dinner.

We come away with the feeling that NATO is best at planning banquets. Fortunately it has never been tested in a big war. They might do well by inviting the enemy to a big banquet and then talking about what they could buy from the enemy—with slides—and, of course, American dollars.

Post script: Margaret Thatcher turns out to be highly successful in reviving England. A big part of her success comes from expanding London into a huge center of world finance, so a lot of people have gone to work in London. She also proves that, maybe she could have effectively run NATO, through her firm defense of the Falkland Islands against Argentina. Of course, The Skooter and I have to visit the Falkland Islands. They don't seem to be worth fighting over. Quite barren, very windy, with only a few brave souls living there speaking English, raising their plants indoors and hopefully surviving the harsh climate. Along with their penguin friends and, of course, tea and crumpets.

Chapter 16

African Cats and Dogs

The Skooter and family always had dogs around, but African wild dogs are something else. They live and hunt in packs with amazing coordination. Every dog has its explicit role in the hunt. We really enjoy watching them go through their paces. It is difficult to be in the right place to see the whole show, but if you can it is a great show. The dogs are wolf-sized and are sometimes referred to as painted wolves because of their remarkable patchwork coloring.

But what The Skooter really loves are the big cats like lions, which already have a chapter in this book. A close second are leopards and cheetahs. On our first trip to Africa, we search for leopards but never see any. On subsequent trips we are more fortunate. Leopards are mostly nocturnal and like to hang out in trees where they have a good view of the situation. They operate by stealth and can move very quickly. After capturing their prey, they like to take it up in the tree for a more private meal.

Some of the very best game parks in the world are in South Africa. Krueger National Park has lots of wild life but it is public and you are restricted to driving on the paved roads. As a result most of what you see is at the watering holes. Krueger Park, however, is surrounded by luxurious private game parks. There are no fences so the animals are free to go back and forth. Leopards like the big trees in these private parks, so most parks provide escorts for their guests when they walk back to their accommodations in the dark after dinner. The Skooter and I are staying at one of these luxury parks and go out on an early morning game run as usual. The driver comes across a leopard who has been hunting all night without making a kill. The leopard is tired, but certainly hungry and a little bit desperate at this point. Our driver charges through the underbrush in pursuit of the leopard and does a remarkable job of driving the open-topped vehicle. I am sitting next to the driver. The leopard only gives us an occasional glance as she continues to hunt. Our vehicle makes so much noise crashing through the underbrush that it would scare away any prey. Maybe the leopard can't figure that out. Anyway when the driver finally gives up the chase he turns to me and says, "If that leopard had decided you were the prey, there wouldn't have been a thing I could do to save you." He had a rifle mounted on the hood of the vehicle but he says the leopard is so quick and agile that he wouldn't even have had time to get the rifle out of its rack.

The Skooter's favorite big cat in Africa is the cheetah, the cat built for speed. No mammal on Earth runs faster. The cheetah can go from zero to 60 miles per hour in just three seconds, but only for short distances. Our first viewing is in the Serengeti where we spot a magnificent mother cheetah sitting on top of a huge ant hill with a couple of her youngsters. She has a great unimpeded view from her perch. Later we see another cheetah making a kill with speed and cunning.

This big cat is in trouble so it lands on The Skooter's "must save" list. The Skooter donates to many animal causes. She is certainly right that the territories of wild animals are being squeezed as more people move in, particularly farmers. The farmers view cheetahs as vermin who constantly raid their livestock. So they are gradually being exterminated across Africa.

A remarkable woman, Dr. Laurie Marker, has decided to save the cheetahs and has established a remote center in Namibia in the heart of cheetah country. Of course, The Skooter says we have to visit her and see what's going on. Our driver somehow finds a long driveway that he thinks may lead into Dr. Marker's place so we head down it, but the car breaks down. He says he will walk ahead alone to see if he can find it and leaves us alone, but we do not see any curious cheetahs. The driver comes back and says it is right and the car starts, fortunately.

Dr. Marker's place is very humble. There are no screens on the windows, so lots of flies join us for lunch. Dr. Marker has been able to attract a number of volunteers from the U.S. and Europe for her project. She spends her time speaking to school children to convince the younger generation that saving the wild cheetah is a plus for Namibia.

She is also trying to convince the farmers that they shouldn't kill the cheetahs. In order to accomplish this, she is breeding special dogs that she will donate to the farmers. The pups grow up with the livestock and instinctively protect them from cheetahs and other predators. Wounded cheetahs are also brought to Dr. Marker for rehab. Some become too tame to be put back in the wild. She brings one out for us to pet, and it is the highlight of our great visit.

We move on to a nearby game park that supposedly has the largest concentration of leopards in the world, but the jungle is thick. We are disappointed that we do not see a single leopard. The animals may be there, but that doesn't mean you will see them.

Chapter 17

A Golfing Trip Ends Up in Fez, Morocco

It is summer time and David Jr. is home from Yale. I am a mediocre golfer at best. David Jr. is young and strong but doesn't have time to play much. We decide to enter our local country club's major event for the first time. It is called the Member—Member. It is a big deal with lots of betting on the outcome. David Jr. is the only one in the club to bet on us to win. I don't think we have a chance so I abstain. The Skooter has not yet started playing golf so she is only mildly interested.

Amazingly, thanks to David Jr.'s clutch shots and long drives, we end up winning the two-day event. The grand prize is a week-long golfing trip to a nice resort in Florida. David Jr. needs cash to sustain his lifestyle at college and is able to convert his share of the trip to cash and also has cash from his winning bet on us. I go off on a business trip thinking The Skooter and I will have a relaxing vacation in Florida soon.

On my return, The Skooter excitedly tells me that she has been able to convert our Florida golfing trip into a trip to Fez, Morocco, and she has been busy planning our route from Madrid south to Fez. Of course there is no comparison in cost, but I do not tell her that. It sounds like a fun adventure, and I will be the driver for the two of us.

Our first visit to Madrid is a delight. We go to a nice restaurant for dinner at 10:00 PM and no one is in the restaurant yet. We enjoy the fine art in the Prado Museum, which is still one of my favorites although the experts would say that it has too many paintings on every wall. Then it is on to Toledo, a city built on a perfect fortress site and which is fun to explore. After Toledo, we decide to head south over the mountains to Cordoba. Unfortunately, I fail to check the gas tank, being used to the frequent gas stations of the U.S. We go for miles and through many tiny villages but no gas stations. The Skooter and I are beginning to think we will be spending the night in the mountains with the sheep herders. The car is stick-shift so I put the clutch out and try to extend every precious drop of gas going down the mountains. The Skooter says not to worry, whatever happens, we will be okay.

Cordoba is the ancient capital of the Moors and as we get closer to it, we find a gas station. The Moors came from North Africa in 711 and conquered most of Spain before being stopped by Charlemagne in what is now France. The Moors were driven out of Spain back into Africa but nowhere was their influence left behind more vividly than in Granada, which is our next most enjoyable walking tour. From there, we follow the route of the retreating Moors south through beautiful little white-washed villages, one of which Christopher Columbus once lived in, and onto Gibraltar, toward our goal of Morocco.

We visit Gibraltar briefly and then take the car ferry to Tangier, Morocco. Only then do I fleetingly wonder if I should be taking the rental car to Africa. Tangier is on the western entrance to the Strait of Gibraltar, the entrance to the Mediterranean. Its strategic location has given it a rich history, with many civilizations dating from the 5th century B.C. What interests The Skooter most is its vivid history as a very active spy center before and during World War II. The Skooter is a big fan of Humphrey Bogart and Lauren Bacall. She has picked out a very special hotel on edge of the souk. It is old and built like a fortress with high walls and only one entrance, a huge ancient wooden gate.

The check-in desk sits just inside another smaller door with a clear view out to the big gate. I ask the man at the check-in desk where I should put the car and he tells me to bring it inside the fort and park it where it can be seen from the desk. Apparently nothing is safe outside the fortress at night. Even though they lock the big gate at night, he says they have had burglars climb over the walls. The place begins to sound more exciting to The Skooter.

Actually this hotel has enormous charm throughout. We check into our room, which is dominated by a huge crystal chandelier. We go down for dinner; the dining room is spectacular. Many chandeliers and all candlelight! There are sinister, conspiratorial-looking characters at every table in the semi-darkness. The Skooter thinks she sees Bogart.

I think I see Sidney Greenstreet and Peter Lorre. All in all, it is a great dinner, imagining spies at almost every table.

The next morning, we make a stop at the Caves of Hercules. More bats than we have ever seen! Then it is on the road to Fez, an ancient city on historic North African trade routes. Fez has been referred to as "The Mecca of the West" and actually consists of two walled medinas or cities, making up one of the largest car-free zones of any city in the world. Our hotel overlooks all this. We decide to get a guide and are we ever glad for that decision. The passages are extremely narrow and we have no idea at any point in time where we are. A number of the local Arabs or Berbers traverse these passages by mules. And then there are many little shops selling most everything. And, of course, the carpet stores. We stop for lunch and have the local delicacy, pigeon pie, which we must eat with our fingers. The whole scene is fascinating, but we are happy we have a guide to get back to the hotel. No doubt this scene stimulates The Skooter to want more, more souks, more adventure, etc.

We head back to Madrid. The roads aren't the greatest, but the traffic is light. We do see a wedding party in a motorcade having a good old time. Where are they going? We make it a point to attend as many Arab weddings as possible, wherever we are. They use gold coins [not real] instead of rice, and the weddings are always very festive and lively. The Skooter and I both love Morocco and vow to return, which we do a number of times. The women wear attractive veils, unlike the leather masks worn in some parts of the Mideast. It is amazing to see how they flirt with only their eyes exposed. The Skooter is not amused.

Chapter 18

Kipling's Burma

The Skooter was always an avid reader, since her childhood, and nothing pleased her more than reading about places and times in the old British Empire, such as Burma. Burma has had a turbulent history going back to the beginnings of The Pagan Empire in 849 AD. Between the 11th and 13th centuries, more than 10,000 Buddhist temples were built in the Pagan region. Over 2,000 of those remarkable temples still exist although all surrounding buildings are gone. Pagan's civilization collapsed in the 13th century under the weight of all those tax-free religious temples and adjacent land. The Skooter wants to see Pagan and as much of Burma as we can. Maybe the intrigue has been heightened by the UN naming Burma as one of the least developed countries in the world in 1987.

We enter the Irrawaddy River Delta in our small boat, on our way to as close as we can get to Rangoon, the largest city and capital of Burma. The delta is clogged with silt so there is no docking. Burma is governed by some sort of military junta so we don't know if we will get permission to enter the country. A large delegation comes by tender to board us. They come with no smiles and empty brief cases, and warnings that we must obey all regulations—and a threat that our rooms may be searched when we leave. A few drinks seem to loosen them up and their brief cases fill with their favorite spirits. Later we learn that they also fill up with US dollars. Anyway it looks like we will be admitted to Burma.

The Skooter had prepared for this trip unlike any before or after, and I don't know why. Maybe her research had convinced her that Burma is really desperate for any luxury goods. She collected the little bottles of perfume and toilet items that she had received on her many first class airline flights and put them in a big bag. I asked her what she

is going to do with those, thinking maybe they would be nice little gift items. No, she said, she intends to sell them.

We get our tender and head ashore. I badly need a battery for my video camera and amazingly enough, on inquiring I locate a camera store. Always, a good approach in a strange third-world country is finding a friendly merchant who speaks good English and wants to sell you something. This merchant had my battery but would not do the transaction in US dollars. He says he depends totally on imports for all his merchandise, so if he were caught he would be out of business. He directs us to the market place where he says we can exchange dollars at a very good rate—legally. In the meantime, The Skooter has found someone who wants to buy all her stuff, and he invites us to a nice little tea house so he can examine all of it. I am apprehensive that the police will swoop in or that he is some sort of undercover agent but he really just wants the stuff and pays her in Burmese money, the value of which I have no idea. I just want to get out of there as fast as possible, which we do. We head right for the market, which is in a very old building that is quite open with a high ceiling, unlike the Arab souks we are used to visiting. The money changers are easily located. I sell some US dollars and go back to buy my batteries while The Skooter shops alone. I find her when I get back and she shows me some interesting antiques, which I bargain for. She decides to be legal and shops later at the government store for her rubies.

We head for the biggest attraction in Rangoon and it is most spectacular: the Shwedagon Pagoda, dazzling with gold. We have to

Above and below: Rangoon

take our shoes off to walk around. Construction on the grounds was started 2,500 years ago. Among many relics are strands of the Buddha's hair. There are hundreds of colorful temples, stupas, and statues around the site. Everything is covered with real sparkling gold plates. The top of the main stupa is encrusted with 4,531 diamonds, the largest of which is 72 carats. The site is called Singuttara Hill and the temples stand as high as 110 meters. Many orange-

Pagan

robed Buddhist monks walking everywhere add to the scene and make the site seem alive. Not too many tourists around!

We take off for more walking around Rangoon. The buildings are old and run-down. No new construction anywhere. No hotels worth staying at. We are scheduled out on Air Burma to Pagan. The airport has very little activity. Our plane is a small two-engine jet that was made a long time ago in Holland. The co-pilot is the steward. Flying into Pagan, we get a great view of the thousands of ancient temples. It is like a ghost city because there is only barren land between the stone buildings that have lasted so long. We land and get a full tour around the site, including a complete history. Finally back to the small little airport, only to find a step-ladder under one of the jet engines. Always curious, I climb into the plane. No one is in the cockpit but a big manual lying on the pilot's seat is open to the chapter on engine malfunctions.

I go back to tell The Skooter that I don't think we are going anywhere, and how would she like to spend the night in a Buddhist temple in Pagan? Then they announce on a loudspeaker to board and I am shocked. I see the co-pilot and ask him what happened. His story is not at all reassuring. He says the engine was stalling out after they started it. So

I asked him how they fixed it since there is no mechanic at this airport. He says "Oh, we just did what you probably do with your car, put the hood up, poke around a bit and put the hood back down."

I thought about getting off the plane with my beloved Skooter but then I wondered how we would ever get back to Rangoon and our boat. I had one bit of knowledge that kept me from totally panicking. To be certified, that plane had to prove that it could take off with one engine and that's what they did. I put my trust in the Dutch engineers.

We successfully return to Rangoon and our boat. Some of The Skooter's friends have been more daring than she and bought rubies and sapphires on the open market, but she is happy. We go to the purser because I want to cash a check, but he has no dollars. I guess the Burmese customs officials are happy because they do not search our rooms.

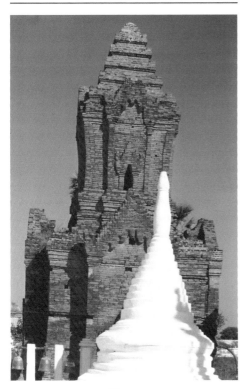

Pagan

Note: I used the names that were being used at the time. Most have been changed for reasons I do not know. Burma, as Myanmar, has rejoined the world and is on an upswing.

Chapter 19

Mongolia—The Land of Genghis Khan

The Skooter had a pony when she was little and then graduated to horses. When we were dating, she took me to horse shows, which I thought were boring—okay, the jumping was interesting. When we got married, she was in tears because she had to sell her horse and leave her German Shepherd behind. In later years, a common joke of mine was that she traded her horse and dog for me and was never quite sure she made a good deal.

Along with raising her 3 boys and volunteer activities, she never had much time for horseback riding, but she took every chance she could. There are some happy memories of us riding together, such as on the deserted beaches south of Acapulco. But she was comfortable in the saddle and I really wasn't, so she alone had the exciting experiences.

Since Genghis Khan and horses combined to form the most thrilling part of Mongolia's history, it is not surprising that Mongolia got on our remote traveling list, in fact, twice, because we didn't cover what we wanted in our first trip. Our flight into Ulaanbaatar is uneventful and the city looks and feels like a tired old Soviet relic. In fact, Mongolia came under Soviet influence in the 1920's and adopted a new constitution only in 1992, with a transition to a market economy. Our hotel is connected to a Soviet era, city-wide, centralized, steam-heating system so our room is unbearably hot from old radiators while it is very cold outside. Open the windows and you combine cold, snow and wind with steam and, of course, it's impossible to get the right combination for comfort. Plus, with the open window, you get the city noises.

Outside of a couple big government buildings and statues, Ulaanbaatar is unremarkable, but the countryside is more interesting. Histori-

cally Mongolians have been nomads and many live in what they call *gers* (yurts), which are frequently moved from place to place. We spend some time in a *ger* and it is very comfortable. The women produce beautiful silk fabrics and they are all dressed up for us. They serve us some if their native drink, which is fermented goat's milk. It has a real kick! Also some hard sweet that would break your teeth if you bit into it. The *gers* are arranged in some sort of community. Goats abound, and some motorcycles, but no horses.

Mongolia is landlocked and remote from populated areas. It is rich in minerals, such as copper, but how to get them developed and marketed is a big problem. Mongolia wants a free market system, which the people believe will solve the problems. But Mongolia is rich in something immediately available that intrigues The Skooter and that is cashmere. It is late in the day but they promise they will take us to the cashmere factory and keep it open as long as we want. We get there and The Skooter is in cashmere heaven. Figuring out what to buy is difficult because the place is huge and the choices wide but we manage. Once back at the hotel it is time for dinner and a unique show featuring amazingly agile, thin Mongolian dancers. The next day we leave, but not without absorbing the legend of Genghis Khan and his horses, and we know we will be back again to this barren land.

Genghis Khan was born near Ulaanbaatar and became King of the Mongols in 1190. He then united with the Tatars in 1206 and started his conquests. His secret was mastery of horses and horsemanship to a degree never seen in the world. Not only were his men the best riders in the world, they were totally self-sustaining. They carried everything they needed to sustain themselves individually so they could ride end-

lessly on their sturdy little horses. The result was an army that was totally mobile and did not have to stop to be resupplied. They could attack swiftly but then move in any direction. Genghis Khan revolutionized warfare with the horse.

Genghis Khan conquered the Xia and Jin Dynasties in China in 1210 and 1215. Then he moved west on what later would be known as The Great Silk Trading Route. He made a brutal conquest of Persia in 1219-21. He became one of the most feared conquerors of all time and became a master of the siege. While he slaughtered many, he was reputed to be very shrewd and always spared the artisans and those who worked with their hands and were needed to keep the economy going. The aristocracy and those he thought didn't do any real work were the ones he eliminated. He is reputed to have ridden all the way to Vienna where he didn't like all the woods and headed back. He encouraged trade and set up the first international postal system. When he died in 1227 his burial

site was kept secret and has still not been found. The Mongol Empire continued under Genghis Khan's sons and grandsons until 1368.

On our second trip we head for the grassland steppes west of Ulaanbaatar. The steppes are great wide open spaces ideal for raising and riding horses. No wonder the Mongolians were so good at horsemanship! The Skooter is really excited to be riding a descendent of one of Genghis Khan's horses. Thrilled, she rides off onto the grassland and I, equally thrilled, watch, with tears in my eyes, as she disappears from view, without a tree in sight.

Chapter 20

The UAE; A New Mid-Eastern Power

Always on the lookout for new places to sell building materials, I had heard that great things are being planned for the United Arab Emirates (UAE) and I have to go see for myself. The UAE is a country located on the southern shore of the Persian Gulf and achieved independence from Britain in 1971. It is a federation that consists of seven emirates: Abu Dhabi, Dubai, Sharjah, Fujarah, Ras al-Khaimah, Umm al-Quwain, and Ajman.

The UAE covers some 400 miles of the southern approaches to the strategic Straits of Hormuz, the only exit and entrance for the Persian Gulf. Saudi Arabia is to the south and Oman to the east. The emirs agreed to rotate the presidency of the UAE.

The area is blessed with a sub-tropical climate with warm winters. It was known to the British in the early 1800's as a pirate coast and also noted for its pearl fisheries. After considerable fighting, the British finally reached a settlement in 1853 known as the "perpetual maritime truce" but the pirating tradition lingered. Bahrain and Qatar, also on the Persian Gulf, decided not to join the UAE. Oil was not discovered in the UAE until the 1950's and by far, the most oil was found in Abu Dhabi, giving that ruler considerable leverage as to where and how the revenues are spent.

My first trip to the area is to Dhahran, Saudi Arabia, headquarters of Aramco and administrative center for the Saudi oil industry. To get there you have to go to Bahrain and take a 15 minute flight to Dhahran. It is amazing what they have accomplished there, but even more amazing what is being planned. A causeway is going to be built to Bahrain, eliminating the 15-minute air flight. Then onto the UAE. Our tiny office is going to be in Sharjah but the enormous building plans are for Dubai. The river runs through the center of Dubai and many old boats, called dhows are docked along its banks. I am told that many of these dhows go back and forth every night to Iran, bringing goods and usually Persian rugs back. The old souk in Dubai is fascinating, particularly the gold section. The walls and ceiling are covered with mirrors. Gold is almost all 24-karat and orange in color so the reflection off the mirrors makes each shop sparkle and glow in an unbelievable way. Arabs from all over the Mid-East come to buy gold. The women hide the gold under their black robes.

In Dubai, I meet with several Arab construction contractors who are most impressive. One I am particularly impressed with tells me he came from Palestine. He says he decided there was no future in Palestine so he moved his whole ready-mix concrete operation to Dubai in a caravan across the desert. Trucks, conveyers, the plant itself, etc. He says these people want to build in peace and have the most stupendous plans he has ever seen. And I could say the same! They are going to desalinate salt water from the Gulf and pump sand for beaches and to create new land. And they are going to build some of the highest concrete buildings in the world. They plan to create their own airlines to bring people to this new paradise. And all with quality construction and real Arab ingenuity.

When I get home and tell The Skooter about all this, you can just imagine the reaction. An emphatic "I'M GOING!!! When I calm her down, I tell her I don't think she will ever get to Saudi because they don't like women. That just raises her level of determination a few notches. I also tell her I think there will be trips to the UAE in the future to see if these Arab dreams materialize. And there are many.

On the first trip for The Skooter to the UAE, she is as excited as I am. Dubai is a huge construction site, but the gold souk has retained its old charm and is busier than ever. Arabs are buying. The Skooter is so dazzled that she can't decide what to buy. We rent a car and go exploring. We head east through undeveloped areas toward Oman and decide to take a swim in the Gulf of Oman. We put Oman on our list for future travel. When we do eventually travel to Oman and its capital Muscat, we find it a delightful place, very clean and safe. Ruled by a benevolent Sultan, Oman has invested its modest oil revenues wisely. They hired

German engineers to build a modern road system. They built at least one luxury hotel that could match any in the world. Anti-litter ordinances keep the streets and sidewalks as clean as any in the world. One thing that does amuse us is that Oman boasts of the largest Mercedes dealership in the world at the time. The Sultan alone reputedly owns 432 for himself and his ministers. The visual picture of the Sultan and his ministers traveling to the little villages in a long caravan of Mercedes to listen to the people amuses us. Certainly different from camels!

On the next trip, The Skooter gets to go along with me. I am working in a different industry, aluminum. It's very much a world-wide industry with many companies owned by governments. Competing with governments is not fun or easy, so my mission is to sell the company in whole or parts. This is not very easy either, because we are losing money and have already announced we are exiting the aluminum business and

Evening Party - International Hotel, Merana, Bahrain

taking a big financial write-off. The Skooter is a good socializer, so perhaps she can help me. And she does as usual.

There are two aluminum companies in the Persian Gulf region, one in Bahrain and one in Dubai. I am president of our U.S. company and, as such, can attend this gathering of aluminum company presidents from all over the world. Bahrain and Dubai compete vigorously to serve as host but Bahrain is selected. Dubai is not to be outdone, so they invite every attendee to come to Dubai at their expense after the meeting in Bahrain. Dubai wants to show that they are the better host. Bahrain is an excellent host and the official meeting goes off well.

Then we are off to Dubai where we are treated like royalty. Everything they are doing in Dubai is amazing and has continued to progress rapidly since we were last there. The aluminum plant is a technical marvel that includes a huge water desalination plant that serves the city for drinking water. They have hired the best architects, engineers and builders in the world for everything they do. There are many receptions, including one at the private home of the president of the aluminum company, who happens to be from England. The gardens make you feel like you are in England, with the exquisite hedges and a marvelous rose garden included in the precise landscaping. If you peek through the hedges, you can see the wide sandy beaches of the Persian Gulf. The Skooter is enthralled by it all.

It is now years later and I am retired. More time for travel, says The Skooter. And, of course, the UAE is on our list, to see how it has developed, and to see Abu Dhabi, which we have never visited. We head to the UAE through Paris, which is our favorite walking city in the world. Our son, Bradley, and his wife, Anne, are currently in Paris. The Skooter is so excited about our trip that she convinces Anne to come along— except for Abu Dhabi.

On the subsequent trip with The Skooter and Anne, our first hotel is actually in Ajman, right

Dubai Skyscraper

on the Persian Gulf with a good sandy beach. The dining room has a menu in Russian as well as English so we guess they attract many Russian tourists. Then it is on to Dubai. Our hotel is unbelievable. A totally enclosed indoor ski slope is part of the complex, as well as a large shopping center. If you are a mom with kids you can drop them off for a little skiing while you go shopping. For our part, we have a drink and dinner while watching the skiers.

The Skooter and Anne are anxious to do some serious sight-seeing and shopping on their own so off they go. One destination is the luxury housing area created by filling in sand in the shape of a palm tree, and its adjoining huge, luxury hotel. We get together to tackle the Sharjah souk. The Skooter goes gold shopping, but Anne is looking for antiques, which I believe have all been picked over by now, at least the real ones. I sit down to read my Wall Street Journal. Anne comes to get me saying she has found a good antique store and wants me to help her negotiate. Truly, she has found a good store and she wants to buy an antique pirate's pistol. The dealer has three antique pistols. They are genuine and beautiful, with mother-of-pearl inlaid in the handles. I negotiate for one, but Anne surprises me by telling me she wants all three, which she proceeds to buy. Then I help The Skooter buy her gold.

When we leave the souk, I ask Anne how in the world she intends to get the pistols home to Florida. That detail is probably why they have remained unsold so long, in spite of their attractiveness. She says she will find a way. When we next see Anne—no pistols. She has mailed them at the Ajman post office—no insurance. But this is the UAE, so, in time, they safely arrive.

The Skooter and I move on to Abu Dhabi. It is unbelievable! The ruler likes greenery so there is green grass everywhere—and trees and bushes as well as palm trees. It is so beautiful that is hard to comprehend. Our hotel is so massive that in three days we still don't know our way around. Not to worry - there are security guards everywhere to ask. Our room—more like a suite—has two huge entrance doors we have to unlock to get in. There are twelve restaurants in the hotel so we have plenty of choices of cuisine, but we do need good directions to find them. For day-time activities there are, of course, beautiful pools, but we elect to go to the new, huge, magnificent mosque that has just opened. It is one of the largest in the world and truly gorgeous. If you want to go to the desert, there are camel races. When the time comes, we hate to leave this fabulous oasis in the desert.

The UAE truly shows what Arab ingenuity can do when concentrated on positive things such as building. What they are doing is such a contrast to the turmoil of the rest of the Middle East. And they are willing to fight to keep the peace. They are now being called "Little Sparta". Abu Dhabi has its own beautiful airport which is where The Skooter and I leave from, and its own airline. But not to be outdone, we hear that Dubai is planning a new airport five times the size of Chicago O'Hare. I played a small part in helping to build O'Hare so I know just how big that is.

Chapter 21

Bears Snag Salmon in Alaska

The Skooter loves all kinds of bears and says she has found the perfect place to see them snag spawning salmon in Alaska. It is Brooks Falls in Katmai National Park, home to the world's largest protected population of grizzlies, called brown bears in coastal Alaska. The park is about 300 miles southwest of Anchorage and accessible only by seaplane. The Skooter wants to convince some of the California Dressler boys to join us and succeeds with son, David Jr. and grandson, David III.

The Skooter and I fly to Anchorage to spend a few days there, which we thoroughly enjoy. Anchorage has a frontier feeling and a new museum to back it up. We get to meet some of the husky dogs that are trained to run in the rugged Iditarod Trail race across Alaska. Then we take our seaplane to the lake adjoining Brooks Lodge. Everybody has

to get a briefing from the rangers. We are told that the park belongs to the bears and that a full-grown 1,000-pound bear can run as fast as a race horse. Don't challenge them. Don't carry any food and avoid eye contact which the bears may regard as threatening. The viewing plat-form at Brooks Falls is about a half mile away. If a bear is blocking the path, retreat—the rangers will not move a bear. The bears always have the right of way.

The Skooter has picked the exact right time in July to make this trip; the salmon are just starting to spawn. We head to the viewing plat-form. The bears below the falls are gorging themselves on the salmon, which are everywhere. No salmon can make the jump up the falls. One lonely bear is sitting at the top of the falls, waiting, but he is not catch-ing anything because the salmon can't make it that high. He should be hungry but he doesn't move. Eventually we have to head back to the lodge but coming down the path towards us is a huge bear and I want to take his picture. How can you do that and avoid eye contact? So I hold my ground and the bear decides to desert the path. I look around behind me for The Skooter, but she is gone—apparently in full retreat as instructed.

Everywhere you go you run into bears of all sizes. But the Dressler boys decide they would rather go fishing. There are so many salmon in the clear water that you could probably pick them out of the water by hand. The Skooter and I want to spend extended time observing the bears from the viewing platform. Things have totally changed from the previous day. My lonely bear at the top of the falls who was not catching anything the previous day is now showing his tremendous athletic ability by picking jumping salmon right out of mid-air with his mouth! Look mom, no hands!

Bears everywhere are gorging themselves, but a new element has been added. American eagles have flown in to enjoy the feast. They hang out in the tall trees and swoop down for a quick salmon treat whenever they want. More and more salmon are successfully making the big jump up the falls and swimming up the river to their spawning grounds.

The next day is still different. The bears are getting saturated with salmon and seem even less interested in the humans around them. The bears are also fussier in what they eat. They prefer the brains and roe and toss the rest of the salmon back in the water. We are mingling more with the bears. I guess human meat can't compare with fresh Alaskan salmon. The eagles continue their treat.

We take time out to do a trek through the Valley of 10,000 Smokes. In 1912, the largest volcanic eruption of the 20th century happened here in Alaska. Later it was named Novarupta. For sixty hours, ash and lava went as high as twenty miles in the air. The lava went down the Ukak River valley at up to one hundred miles per hour. The river valley transformed into forty square miles of ash and lava, which today you can hike over. Trapped water led to superheated steam escaping from vents, hence the Valley's name.

On Sunday, our seaplane is scheduled to pick us up at 1:00 p.m. The Skooter goes down to the viewing platform for one last session with the bears. The plane arrives and picks up our bags, but no Skooter. It seems Mama Bear and her cubs didn't want The Skooter to leave so they planted themselves in such a way as to block the path back. We frantically ask the rangers what we can do and they say, "Nothing until the bears decide on their own to move." The lodge is sold out so I have visions of sleeping on a couch in the lobby. We had already been very cramped with four people in our little cabin. Fortunately, the pilot did not seem in any great hurry to leave. Eventually The Skooter shows up. The bears had decided to move. And so we were able to take off for Anchorage and home.

Chapter 22

Beautiful South America— With Lots of Inflation

Beautiful scenery, fun-loving people, and lots of activity. Over the years, The Skooter and I take it all in, except for Bolivia. Over a period of time, I was responsible for business operations in three South American countries: Brazil, Columbia, and Venezuela. All three operations were very difficult to manage because of currency inflation that often was close to out of control. Recently the world seems to be more and more concerned with deflation but no one seems to be consulting with South America and its long history of inflation. I have always associated inflation with bad governmental policies and certainly that seems to have been true in South America.

Whether it is business trips or just exploring, The Skooter enjoys it all. Not as much animal activity as in Africa, but The Skooter does fall in love with the llamas and at one point insists that we should get one for our back-yard. I have a difficult time convincing her that that wouldn't work with her German Shepherds. The Amazon River trip is actually a disappointment. The river is very wide at its mouth and there is jungle on both sides so you don't see much. When the river gets narrower and you make shore excursions, you see a lot of monkeys and not much else, other than interesting native tribes.

Our company plant is in Rio de Janeiro, a very large and lively city with beautiful beaches and hotels. Brazil was discovered way back in 1565 by the Portuguese. One of the charming features of Rio is the huge statue of Christ The Redeemer at the entrance to the harbor. One of the not so nice features of Rio is its historical high crime rate. The workers taking the bus to and from our plant were robbed regularly on pay day—one year 52 times. I had to warn the fearless Skooter not to wear jewelry or take a purse if she went to the beach. Since inflation was so high, you tried to convert your depreciating paper money into something of real value as fast as possible. Criminals knew that too, so they robbed condo complexes often. With a gun to your head, you will open your safe. (With the Olympics coming as I write this, Brazil is confronting some of its nagging problems. The country is rich in resources and talented people.)

Since our plant in Brazil has plenty of capacity, I decide to take The Skooter along on a business exploratory trip to Argentina. Argentina is such a gorgeous country. It has everything going for it: a temperate climate, well- educated resourceful people, rich farmland, and lots of natural resources. Buenos Aires has long been called the Paris of South America and rightfully so because of all its charm and lively night action. My first order of business is meeting with government leaders in charge of investment. My first question is, "What is your current yearly rate of inflation?" The answer is "100%." Instinctively I say "That's awful." Surprisingly, they say, "No, it is wonderful; last year it was 300%." The meeting goes on but my decision is made.

I go back to the hotel and tell The Skooter that there is no way I will go home and recommend any investment in Argentina so I will not be tied up in business meetings. "This place is worse than Brazil. They do not understand the adverse effect inflation has on business investment. We will just have a good time in this lovely spot." And we do.

The local people claim they invented the tango so the first night we see some really fantastic performances of that wild dance. The next night it is the opera in a beautiful old opera house. Argentinians eat dinner later than anywhere in the world and they love their steak and potatoes. They produce some of the finest beef in the world. On Tuesday evening we go to a restaurant for a huge and delicious dinner. We leave the restaurant at 2:30 a.m., and the restaurant is still half-full. Our friends say they will pick us up at the hotel in the morning at 8:30 a.m. After a couple days of this we try to figure out when they sleep because there is no afternoon siesta. They say they feed the kids at 6:00 p.m. Our guess is that they have a siesta from 7:00 to 9:30 p.m. or so and then go out to dinner. It was the only open time on our schedule. The last day, they took us out to the countryside and a horse ranch. The Skooter was

Doing the Amazon

especially delighted. We had a scrumptious afternoon tea in this pleasant outdoor setting.

Columbia is another wonderful stop. We are a little apprehensive because the country is having serious problems with the drug cartels, but our hosts have excellent security. They tell us never to wait to be picked up outside the hotel, always in the lobby. The first day my boss and I are taken on a tour of Columbian industry and The Skooter gets to go to the fabulous gold museum with the ladies. Our hosts take us to the family compound for dinner that night with cars of armed security in the front and behind. The dinner is a Spanish delight and after dinner I lament the fact that The Skooter got to see all these fabulous Incan gold relics while I only got to see cement mills. Our host says to wait a minute while he exits. When he comes back he has several old shoe boxes. He starts to unwrap objects from the boxes and they turn out to be priceless gold relics that I get to hold in my hands and closely examine. They had been found on our host's flower plantations.

The next day we are taken by helicopter to see more of Columbia's industry and countryside. The Skooter gets to go see the fantastic flower plantations our hosts own. Columbia produces some of the best flowers grown anywhere in the world and exports huge quantities to Europe and the U.S. As dusk descends and the clouds move in, our helicopter maneuvers around the mountains toward our destination, a coffee plantation where a reception is planned for us. The lack of visibility makes the ride a little scary but we make it. Columbia produces some of the best coffee in the world. The trees are meticulously groomed. The U.S. ambassador arrives. His car is so heavily armored with steel plate that it has overheated and is spouting smoke. All in all, it is another memorable evening. From all I see and hear, I am optimistic about Columbia's future. They understand how the business world works and are trying to control inflation and solve their problems.

Venezuela is another story. Same wonderful Spanish hospitality so The Skooter enjoys it immensely, but they have long pursued unwise economic policies. Over the years, I am involved in both the steel and aluminum industries. Venezuela is very rich in natural resources and has huge oil reserves, bauxite for aluminum, and iron ore for steel. As their economists explain it to me, all these resources are really free because otherwise they would just lie in the ground unused. Energy is free also, except for extraction costs, and labor is free also since their people need to be put to work. By their calculations they are the low-cost producer in the world. The government sells gasoline way below world prices and so everyone can buy a second-hand car, but then there are not enough parking places in Caracas. When it rains, the old cars break down and there is chaos. The government solution: build huge concrete parking garages but only charge about 15 cents a day, not nearly enough to cover costs. Add to that the custom agents demand for tips. My solution is to hold board meetings in Miami which pleases everyone. Everyone in Latin America loves Miami. The end comes when the government doesn't pay us for our goods and services and the joint venture dissolves.

To end this chapter on a high note, while others are struggling with inflation, little Chile is solving problems and controlling inflation. The Skooter and I journey through Chile on our way to a boat trip to Antarctica and like what we see. It is put on our "to return" list.

We head to Antarctica through Punta Arenas, Chile, across the rough Magellan Strait. Memorable is a hike along the beach in a snowstorm with strong winds. On the beach are what look like big rocks covered with snow. But wait, the rock nearest us moves slightly. It is actually a seal hunkered down in a ball with its back to the wind riding out the storm. We also see lots of penguins, sea lions, walruses, and other wild life adapted to this harsh environment. We are told that there are only two green things growing in Antarctica—-both wild grasses. We don't see them.

Chapter 23

In Search of Tigers—
Nepal and India

Nepal was a small, unstable monarchy when we first visited, but it was colorful. Located high in the Himalayas, Kathmandu is an interesting city to explore but The Skooter senses another opportunity—-finally a chance to see tigers in the wild. Tigers need big territories and the parks that can contain them are becoming rare as civilian populations expand and encroach in both Nepal and India. The Skooter finds a terrific lodge for us where we are sure to see tigers because they bait to bring them in. We are having cocktails when they ring the bell that the tiger has arrived and we all get up for a look-see. Beautiful animal, a

teen-ager we are told, and very powerful and graceful. It doesn't take him long to rip apart and devour the goat.

The next morning we are to ride elephants through the jungle in search of tigers. The Skooter and I and another stranger are put on one elephant. It is too much for the elephant, and someone has to move since the saddle is slipping and we all may fall off. I am elected and it is an amazing process. The elephant kneels and with his trunk, forms a slide for me so I can easily slide to the ground. The new elephant curls his tail to form a step which I climb on and then boost myself over the elephant's rump and crawl up to the saddle.

We are off into the jungle when I drop my camera's lens cover onto the jungle floor. The mahout, our driver for the morning, commands the elephant to pick it up, which the elephant promptly does and hands it to me with his trunk. I couldn't even see where it had been in the dense jungle underbrush.

The elephant ride is very smooth, unlike a camel. But suddenly the elephant makes a huge jump into the air with all four feet. We are startled; then we see a mother rhino with a little baby rhino charging our el-

A gharial

ephant. We had always heard that in the law of the jungle size mattered, and the larger animal prevailed, but in this case, protection of young prevailed. Anyway it was a mock charge, just sending the elephant a message—don't mess with my kid. We trudged through the jungle all morning without flushing out a tiger, prompting me to ask our guide how often he had seen a tiger in the daytime. He said just twice all year.

The next camp we go to is a small, tented camp on the river. We see the rare, fish-eating crocodile called a *gharial.* They grow up to 20 ft. and have a long snout with 110 sharp teeth. Our little tent is at the end of a row and furthest from the main facilities. We note that the other tents are unoccupied. The Skooter loves tent living and sleeps like a log but I do not and will be thinking about *gharials* and tigers coming out of the river up to our tent. Bengal tigers are great swimmers and are known to upset villagers' fishing boats for a tasty meal—the fisherman, not the fish he caught.

We go to cocktails and are the only ones there outside of a party of six Aussies who had brought along a supply of Dom Perignon. No, they didn't offer us any. The bell rang and there are the tigers. What a sight! A mother tiger and two little ones. It s a truly fantastic viewing as mom helps herself and gives the leftovers to the kids. It doesn't take them long.

The night is long but quiet and I do not wander from the tent. No tigers or gharial come to visit.

Pushkar Camel Fair

Nepal suffered from an insurgency during our visit. In 2008 the Nepalese voted to oust the monarchy.

India was one of The Skooter's real favorites. She loved the color and the pomp left over from the days of The British Empire. India was and still is a land of great contrasts: New Delhi, the beautiful capital with its broad streets and parks, and Old Delhi with its squalor, poverty and cramped dirty quarters. There are fantastic sights to see, like The Taj Mahal, a white marble mausoleum built in Agra by Mughal Shah Jahan in 1632. It is considered the jewel of Muslim art in India. Its Mughal architecture combines Islamic, Persian, Ottoman Turkish, and Indian influences. A must see!

The Skooter and I continue our search for tigers in India but it is discouraging. Indian game parks are run by the government and are lacking in good accommodations, and when we are there, lacking in tigers. The Skooter persists and tells me she has found the perfect spot for tigers in India—Kanha. Only one problem — it is an eight-hour drive from nowhere over narrow, bad roads to get there. I have had bad experiences with Indian roads and my back.

She finds two friends who want to go and I stay home. Bad decision! They have a fantastic trip and see tigers from the backs of elephants and from vehicles. The Skooter is really thrilled over the success of the trip. I am pleased that the Indian govern-

Skooter in Katmandu, Nepal

125

ment seems to be doing something right to save these beautiful creatures in the wild. No baiting.

The Skooter makes many trips to India and loves every one. I enjoy it too, but must admit I am somewhat taken aback by the poverty and lack of proper sanitation. I am told that tax money is collected to clean the streets, for example, but it doesn't get done. Indians are bright, resourceful people, so I am hopeful they will find good ways to make real progress. The Skooter makes some trips without me, so I miss out on some of her favorites. One of these is Jaipur, called the Pink City of India because of the color of the stone with which it was constructed beginning in 1727. It has some magnificent gates, among other features. Another place she really enjoys is The Pushkar Camel Fair, held every November. She stays in a tent, which she thinks is just great because she is surrounded by so many camels and there is so much action and commotion day and night. She does add that she is the only one in her group that thinks it is great—-the others all object to the awful smells from all the camels.

Chapter 24

Tracing the Path of the Vikings to North America

While The Skooter liked camping out, she also liked the luxury of a good cruise ship, which I preferred, so we went on many interesting cruises exploring the world. We decide to take one tracing the path of the Vikings when they discovered North America at L'Anse aux Meadows in what is now Newfoundland.

The Vikings were at their peak in the 8th to the 11th centuries. These Germanic Norse seafarers had amazing sailing skills and built the most advanced ships of the time. They traveled far and wide in their longboats, which were primarily fighting ships, and knarrs, which were designed more for commercial use. The Vikings raided and pillaged but also were great traders. There is evidence that they went as far as Bagdad to trade.

We start our journey in Copenhagen, a charming city with a great port. From there we sail to Bergen, an old very active port in Norway. At Bergen we learn a lot about The Hanseatic League, a group that dominated sea trade from 1250 to 1500. Bergen was a key member. The Vikings used their ships in many different ways: sometimes tactically they buried a ship to block a harbor and sometimes they used them as burial sites. Amazingly, some of these ships have been found, raised from the sea and resurrected, and now reside in museums. Very sturdy!

We head north from Norway along the coast of Scotland to the Faroe Islands. In the 9th century, the Vikings had a significant settlement here, which we visit. The Faroes are north of Scotland and have a variable climate influenced by the Gulf Stream. It is said that the Faroes are the only place in the world where you can experience all four seasons in the same day. It is very windy and the Viking site is treeless but the homes were built of stone and securely anchored into the ground. You apparently could go from one building to another without going outside, but it would certainly be rugged living.

While on the subject of the Faroes, I have to tell the story of a very talented piano player we met, who was born there. Not only was he born there, but he insisted he could remember it all, including coming down the birth canal in childbirth. Since The Skooter and I cannot remember anything much before age four, this story did seem open to challenge, but he strongly stuck by it. Maybe there is something really unique about the Faroes!

Iceland was reportedly discovered by a Viking who got very lost coming out of the Faroes. The Vikings apparently did not know what they had in Iceland, with its volcanoes and geothermal springs, so they tried to keep it a secret from the rest of the world. In the late 9th century, they started to send settlers. The Viking boats included men, women, children, and farm animals, so you can imagine what the long arduous journey must have been like. Nevertheless, the Vikings established a solid, self-sustaining colony with cattle and sheep. They were probably the first to enjoy the warm thermal baths in the very dark winters.

Viking history was chronicled in The Sagas. The first permanent settler came to Iceland in 874 and was named Arnarson. He called the settlement Reykjavik, which is the name of Iceland's present capital city. The Skooter and I enjoy exploring every bit of Iceland. Reykjavik proves to be an active, colorful city. As we found with almost all northern climes, the people enjoy hard liquor and good companionship.

As the story goes, a Viking named Eric The Red got in some big trouble with the colony and either decided to leave or was kicked out. He decided to go west to Greenland and establish his own colony. Naming the place Greenland no doubt enhanced his ability to attract other colonists. They took sheep with them. Eric had a son named Leif Ericson. He decided to head south and tried to establish a colony in what is now Newfoundland. He called it Vinland. The thought that you could raise grapes there, which could lead to wine-making obviously, had appeal to those enduring the cold of Greenland. Leif Ericson was born around 970 so you can see that this was long before Christopher Columbus discovered North America.

Iceland

Adding to all this was the fact that my alma mater, Yale, was given a map called the Vinland Map, whose authenticity became most controversial. I am also a modest map collector so I have read all about it. It is also necessary, to make all this work, to envision that this period of history was enjoying (from the Vikings standpoint) some global warming, which eventually reversed and made the colony in Greenland uninhabitable.

The Skooter and I are excited that our ship is on its way to Greenland and then Vinland. Will we be impressed by what remnants the Vikings have left behind so long ago? Will we become believers that the Vikings really were the ones that deserve credit for discovering America?

The Skooter and I are going into dinner with friends when we pass a nautical map charting our course. We are near the spot where the Titanic went down and so many lives were lost. I tell The Skooter not to worry; this is late fall and not iceberg season. We are eating dinner and suddenly "BOOM" — and people, dishes, food, and chairs go flying in all directions. What did we hit? It can't be an iceberg! The captain turns

A storm in the Atlantic

the ship around to face east and I think, isn't it nice that he did that so we can continue dinner. Then comes the announcement that we were hit by a huge rogue wave and are taking on water in the lower deck. There is some panic, but mostly people are relatively calm. The captain finally announces that they are containing the water entering the lower level; he is evaluating the damage and will decide if we have to go back to Norway for repairs.

Being very curious people, The Skooter and I have to go below to inspect the damage. Apparently, we hit a huge 80-100 ft. rogue wave that was the leading edge of a massive storm—the perfect storm caused by a front coming from the Arctic, combining with a front coming up from the south. The wave went right over the ship taking the bow Jacuzzi with it and smashing the bulkhead door, which is where we are taking on water.

They are already initiating repairs by welding a huge steel plate where the bulkhead door had been. Mostly crew on this level of the ship and their shoes and socks are floating around in water. I tell The Skooter that it gives me great confidence that they have such a huge steel plate and are able to put it in place so quickly to keep the water out.

Neither The Skooter nor I have ever been seasick, so we don't miss a meal or cocktail hour, but many of our fellow passengers are confined to their rooms. The crew does an excellent job of taking care of us because it is really rough. Waves are still coming right over the ship. I tell The Skooter that there is no way we could ever use the lifeboats because we couldn't get to them. At one point, the ship's photographer wants to get some shots. When we open the door, with great difficulty, it takes three men to hang on to her so she isn't blown or washed away. Even so I don't think she got any shots—at least we never saw any.

The Captain made the decision to ride out the storm and headed into the wind with low power so we went up and down in the huge waves like a cork, essentially going nowhere for over two days. Our faith had to be in our Norwegian captain and the Norwegian-built ship (the good Viking heritage). Finally the storm abated and then the bad news. We would have to skip both Greenland and Vinland and limp into St. John in Canada for repairs. We had to evacuate the ship and were broken up into smaller groups to stay on dry land.

The natives were happy for the unexpected tourists and treated us very well. Finally we were headed straight for New York, without any further knowledge, or better opinions, on whether the Vikings actually

were the first to discover America, but glad to be alive to ponder the question.

The Skooter and I had never before gone into New York harbor this way, right by the Statue of Liberty. It is such an impressive sight, welcoming us back. Our friends from New York point out all the sights and we are very happy to be home. That night we celebrate by listening to some great jazz in Greenwich Village.

Chapter 25

A Rising China

The first visit The Skooter and I have to mainland China is an offshoot of a trip to Hong Kong, which is independent at the time. We are in Hong Kong for the Chinese New Year celebration. It is great fun! The parade is awesome, so colorful and lively! Everything shuts down for New Year's, but on another day we ask a local business associate to take us to a "real" Chinese restaurant for dinner. The restaurant serves mainly unpeeled shrimp and chicken, and we are the only non-Chinese in the place. Everybody is eating with their fingers, but what is remark-

able is that when they finish, whether it is a shrimp skin or a chicken bone, everyone just throws it on the floor. No one cleans up so when we leave, the restaurant floor is a mass of litter.

When we go over to Canton, we have to deal with the officious border guards and border police. After delays for unknown reasons, we are cleared. We are dismayed by the amount of litter everywhere— cigarette butts, candy wrappers, whatever—everything gets tossed on the ground. Compared to Japan, which we have visited several times, the contrast is great. Canton holds a world trade fair, so we expect more.

Our next visit is much more interesting. We go to Beijing at a time that just happens to be shortly before the Tiananmen protests. Everything seems calm at The Gate of Heavenly Peace. Thousands of Chinese are riding their bicycles. The sky is clear and bright and everything moves at a slow pace. Beijing has so many fascinating and historic sights that we have trouble covering it all. The Forbidden City is a great attraction. We want to go to a real Chinese restaurant for dinner of Peking duck and it is very different from Hong Kong. The restaurant has naked bright light bulbs and oilcloth on the tables. The service is terrible—no tips—and the food not good. Nobody seems to care about anything. At 7:30 PM, they announce they are closing for the evening.

But there are contrasts and signs that things are changing. Our new western-style hotel is a delight. We are served by young, attentive, attractive Chinese girls so it makes me think of Bangkok. When we are leaving the hotel in the morning, hundreds of older Chinese are coming in and we have to find out what is going on because these people are humbly dressed, do not speak English, and obviously are not business people. They have been invited to a seminar put on by the hotel to explain to the parents of their new work force just what their children will be doing in their new jobs. What a great idea!

The Great Wall turns out to be a most interesting tourist spot. On the way back we stop for lunch at the Beijing Country Club where the greens are covered by white plastic because it is winter. Change is in the air everywhere, but we do not pick up any real hints that a confrontation like Tiananmen Square is just around the corner.

The Skooter wants to go to Tibet and the Chinese don't make it easy. The railroad isn't open yet, but it is impossible to fly right into

The Great Wall

Lhasa which is our destination. Instead we must fly to Chengdu and change to a Chinese plane with lots of people and some rather obvious security agents. We almost did fly right into Chengdu literally, but the pilot made a quick climb and avoided disaster. As we get off the plane,

Tibet, photos above and on next page

thankfully, we ask our pilot what happened. He said he was given the wrong coordinates and in the dark he said he recognized downtown Chengdu when we were about to hit it.

We walk around downtown Chengdu, but aren't very impressed. That evening, I get violently sick (The Skooter would never get sick no matter where we are). I take my Cipro and hope it works. (Always a good idea when traveling remote places to have some antibiotics with you.) No dinner, and by morning I am groggy but able to go. Lhasa is at 11,450 ft. but it seems higher and they provide oxygen in our room. The town is primitive and the Potala Palace looms large over everything. Lots of Buddhist monks walking around, so we go to a monastery as well as to the Palace, which is well worth a thorough tour. Then into the center of town for a walking tour on our own to talk with as many people as we can. Surprisingly, the merchants are all Chinese. The Buddhists have been pushed aside. We are told there are 200,000 Chinese troops in barracks outside town. The Chinese must want this known, true or not, to suppress any thought of rebellion. The Buddhists we see do not seem capable of any uprising. On our way back to China, The Skooter says we should have planned to go see the panda bears out of Chengdu. The Chinese take very good care of their pandas so that takes some careful advance planning.

Over the years, we take several more good trips to China and, wow, is it changing! Cars have replaced bikes. New roads, new buildings are everywhere. Some of the endless new, boxy apartment houses aren't full and aren't very attractive, but some of the new buildings are spectacular. China holds The Olympics and the stadium is an architectural marvel. Shanghai is an architectural blend of old and new and holds a terrific World's Fair. Shanghai has become a booming commercial world business center. And Beijing is now huge but has managed to maintain its charm.

The negative of all this boom is that the electric power is supplied by constant building of coal-fired power plants, and the air quality has become foul. Where is the sun and bright blue sky of the China we once knew? And the water quality isn't too good either. But China is cleaner on the ground than we once knew it, and the Chinese are bright people so The Skooter and I are hopeful they will find effective ways to solve their pollution problems.

Skooter in Tibet

Chapter 26

Thailand and French Indochina

This was one of the favorite areas for The Skooter and me to explore and enjoy. Bangkok has a major international air terminal and some of the best hotels in the world for food and service. In fact, our favorite hotel was consistently rated the best hotel in the world for service. We liked to stay in a semi-suite in the old section, and I will describe only one of their little service tricks that we saw only there. A service employee was assigned to cover our room 24 hours a day. Whenever we were in the room, this employee put a toothpick propped up against our door. When we left the room, of course, the toothpick would fall flat and they would know they could come in and service the room without disturbing us. The outdoor buffet along the river was enormous and very elegant, as was everything else.

Thailand is unique in Southeast Asia because it is the only country that avoided European colonial rule. It was called Siam originally. The

Thailand

Luang Prabang, Cambodia

word "Siamese" is in a 12th century inscription at the Khmer temple complex at Angkor Wat in Cambodia. The Siamese fought many wars, particularly with the French, until the British and French decided that Siam should be neutral territory to avoid conflicts between their colo-

nies. Siam was ruled by a king and was invaded by the Japanese in 1941. After the end of absolute monarchy in 1932, Thailand endured almost 60 years of military rule before establishment of a democratic system, which has at times not functioned smoothly, with what is supposed to be a largely ceremonial king in the background.

As you can imagine, there is lots to explore in Thailand and The Skooter loves it all. Bangkok is a shopper's paradise. To the south, there are the resorts and beautiful beaches of Phuket. The old palace complexes and other temples in and around Bangkok are well worth some time. But no doubt, The Skooter became most excited when we head north of Chiang Mai to visit a big elephant camp. The picture on the cover of this book of The Skooter in the arms of a young elephant was taken there. Elephants are the largest land animals on earth. At birth, a baby elephant weighs 200 pounds and is weaned in 2-3 years. They are herbivores and can eat 300 pounds of food a day. One of their favorites is stripping bark from trees, which is hard on the forests when elephants are overpopulated. Elephants' natural life span is 30 to 50 years in the wild. In some areas they are extensively poached for their ivory tusks.

Asian elephants are slightly smaller than African elephants, but extremely intelligent. All elephants are good swimmers and love to cool themselves with their trunks. But that isn't all they can do with their trunks. Historically, Asian elephants were the work-horses of the economy, doing jobs such as moving logs. The Skooter and I are amazed to see that elephants in northern Thailand have been trained to paint oil pictures of all sorts of things. They hold the paint-brush in their trunk and get the paint from a palette just like an artist would. The paintings are actually quite good. The elephants put on a little show for us, give us a ride through the jungle, and when it is all over they are set free and allowed to go down to the river and splash around, just like a bunch of kids.

The French may not have been able to conquer Siam, but they certainly had a big influence on Southeast Asia. The French were involved in the area as early as the 17th century as traders. French Indochina was formed in 1887. They took Laos from Siam in 1893. In the turmoil of World War II, the Viet Minh under Ho Chi Minh started a revolution. Under the Geneva Accord of 1954, Vietnam was split with the anti-communist State of Vietnam ruling the south out of Saigon and the Viet Minh ruling the north out of Hanoi. Ho Chi Minh had defeated the French but the United States stepped in to support the south. Ho Chi Minh was a popular leader and eventually the United States withdrew.

Knowing The Skooter's perhaps sublime desire to be in and around present and future war zones, I knew we would head to Vietnam in our world travels. To us, it seems that the south had won the war, which they had actually lost. Hanoi is a very interesting city with a strong French influence. Everybody is riding bicycles. Some of the buildings are painted colorfully, as though you are in the south of France. When we get to Saigon, which is now called Ho Chi Minh City, everything is bustling and livelier, but people ride motorbikes, not bicycles. The only building that looks disastrous is the American Embassy that is closed and boarded up with a chain-link fence around it. The city is very active and seems prosperous.

Of course, there are other parts of French Indochina and we had to visit them all. Little Laos seems to have regained its peace and tranquility. A good place to visit. Most tourists go to Cambodia to visit Angkor Wat, which was built in the 12th century as a Hindu temple. Huge stone blocks were used in its construction and it is now believed that the stones were moved from the quarry to the construction site by a series of canals. I would like to believe that Asian elephants played a major role in the construction. Angkor Wat is well preserved. It supported a large and prosperous civilization. As one of the wonders of the world, it

Laos

attracts lots of tourists, and even though the site is large, it can at times become crowded.

The Skooter wants to see more of living Cambodia than just the ruins of Angkor Wat, so we head to Phnom Penh where the Khmer Rouge and Pol Pot attempted to remove Cambodia from the modern world and establish an agrarian utopia in 1975-79, killing at least 1.8 million Cambodians. Phnom Penh is a strange place to visit. The King had cooperated in the whole scheme, so the palace and grounds are preserved in all their splendor. Some of the city is being rebuilt and the population almost exclusively consists of young people. Talking with some of these young people provides gruesome details of what happened. The men were mostly just killed. Children were separated from their mothers and all were sent to rural areas to be re-educated. Memorials have been constructed of human skulls to honor all those who died in the "killing fields". The total population of Cambodia dropped to 1.9 million in 2008 but then rapidly rose as normalcy returned.

Chapter 27

In Search of Roots

There are many luxurious ways to travel around the world, but none quite as superb as the trips described as "first class tours by private jet". I have purposely tried not to mention specific names of hotels, restaurants, etc. because, what may be great for one trip may not work so well on another. But for every rule there is an exception and mine is National Geographic, which has certainly stood the test of time in so many ways. The magazine they publish is just great. The Skooter got many of her exotic travel ideas from them and accumulated the magazines in our attic. She had no indexing system so I always kidded her that if we wanted something on a specific area she would never be able to find it. Her answer: "Just try me."

We are also fortunate to live in Washington D.C., which is the headquarters of National Geographic, so we benefited from their museum and the regular lectures and programs they put on. They sponsor explorers all over the world and provide lecturers for their private jet tours. The one trip that we took that I am going to cover was entitled "Tracing the Human Genome" and had Spencer Welles as the main lecturer. We went around the world and it was one trip where we did not want the 6-7 hour flights to end because the lectures are so great. Welles used DNA to trace the historic migrations of mankind out of Africa and around the world and had accumulated extensive research all over the world.

Long, long ago our human ancestors started out of Africa, where they originated, and headed north into the Middle East, where branches went east, west and north, eventually spreading around the whole world and in the process developing adaptations to various environments throughout the world. Skin pigmentations adapted to various climates through mutation, for example. We visit many historic sites in our journey and hear many others described and pictured on slides. The Lascaux cave paintings in France, which are 16,000 years old, were particularly impressive, but many such sites are now severely restricted for preservation. DNA has opened a whole new window for tracing and analysis of ancient mankind, and much continuing work is going on all over the world.

When we return from The National Geographic trip, The Skooter and I have to get our DNA tested. It turns out that her ancestors wandered around Africa longer than mine before heading out through the Middle East and then to Europe. We had been told in our lectures that women typically moved around more than men, based on DNA tracings. Make your own theory as to why. In my case, my ancestors went through what is now Germany and into southern England. That is consistent with what little we know about family history. I am told that my DNA is the same as a high percentage of men today in southern England. The family history is in Saxony Germany, but history has Saxons fighting in England.

I have one sister, Janet, with whom I am very close. We compare notes on what we know on family history. Our grandfather came to the U.S. as a young man from Kaltensundheim in Saxony, after his brother John. His mother's maiden name was Marianna Bach. Janet with husband Chuck and I with The Skooter decide to take a trip to Germany to trace what we can.

We check a few spots on other relatives and head for Kaltensundheim, which for years after World War II was mired behind the Iron Curtain and only recently became part of a reunited Germany. We stay in a nice hotel that once was in West Germany and drive through what once was the border, and arrive in Kaltennordheim, which looks very rundown. The Skooter insists we stop at the local Lutheran Church where she learns about some of the Dresslers in town, including a talented woodcarver. Of course, we must go to his house and workshop, socialize with his family, order a family coat of arms and a German Shepherd carving, all without any of us understanding the others' language to any extent.

All well and good, but our real objective is Kaltensundheim, and it is now noontime and city hall in Germany shuts down at noon. Besides no one speaks English. Finally, a wonderful young man who is trying to arrange a bicycle tour of Saxony comes to our aid. He says, "You have to see the Lutheran minister," and he takes us there. But he does much more than that. He convinces the minister, in German, that we are worth talking with. The minister invites us in to his library and when he learns what we are looking for he is extremely helpful.

There is a very long history of Dresslers in his church and they have historically been very active. He takes us on a tour of the church, which is very old and very attractive. He proudly shows us the baptismal font where, he says, our grandfather Dressler was baptized. Once back in his office, he pulls out all sorts of old books, some written in old German, but all full of information on generations of Dresslers. My sister and I are frantically taking notes and trying to keep up with what generation was doing what. He even hits such details as who baked the communion bread. The Lutheran Church obviously was a center of social and musical activity, and this minister is very proud of the role the Church played in Kaltensundheim, and for that matter the role that Dresslers played in the Church.

After our exhilarating visit with the minister, we take a quick tour of the very small town, which frankly looks like something out of the

The Dressler Woodcarvers

Bach Haus Museum

1930's. Buried behind the Iron Curtain after World War II, it just hasn't changed. The town, however, does have a small museum, which we visit. What impresses me the most is the memorial they have to soldiers killed in World War I and another for World War II. This tiny town contributed an awful lot of men to the wars and, of course, there were Dresslers, Bachs, and other relatives.

Saxony was sandwiched between warring German states and home to such intellectuals as Martin Luther and Johann Sebastian Bach. In 1871, Bismarck is quoted as saying he would unite Germany through "blood and iron". I was and am so proud that my grandfather, as a very young man with nothing, had the guts to escape and start an American Dressler branch of the family.

As part of our trip, we go to Eisenach, the birthplace of Johann Sebastian Bach, and visit the Bach Haus Museum, which proves to be a real delight. They actually play the antique instruments every hour, and the music is not only authentic but sounds great.

The Skooter and I return to our home in the Washington D.C. suburbs. Over the years, we have had access to almost all the foreign embassies. At one time, the German cultural attaché was a good friend and we went to many musical programs in her house and at the embassy. The embassies certainly stimulated our desire to travel the world. The Germans maintain an excellent school, mostly for the children of their diplomats, but open to anyone. It is there that I go to see if I can get some help in translating my copious notes. The librarian there could not have been nicer. She even took some of the more difficult words, such as "zwoelfer" home to get her husband's opinion.

One last follow-up. I buy a detailed genealogy book on Johann Sebastian Bach, written in German, and am able to trace the Bach roots way back, despite more than one Marianna Bach and the book's emphasis on tracing male descendants. From best I can tell, the Kaltensundheim Bachs are from the Rhoner Bach stem (whatever that means). My best guess is that the Kaltensundheim Bachs were like country cousins to the more urban Eisenach Bachs, although they all loved their music, which was ingrained in Saxony.

Chapter 28

Unique Japan

As a collector of antique maps, I am fascinated by seeing Japan all over the Pacific Ocean in the maps. The reason is that early mapmakers depended on returning ships for information and often Japan was excluded from such visits. From the 12th century till the 1850's, Japan was ruled by feudal shoguns in the name of the Emperor. In 1853, Japan was pressured to open up to the world. Lacking oil and other natural resources, Japan reached out to neighbors to secure them, sometimes by force. Despite a number of wars, Japan today has the highest life expectancy of any country in the world, or so I've been told.

Over the years I have been responsible for two joint ventures with Japanese partners: one in which our U.S. side had a 50% interest in the Japanese company and another in which the Japanese had a 35% interest in our U.S. company. As a result, I got to know the Japanese quite well. I made a number of trips to Japan, some with The Skooter and some without. 50-50 joint ventures are difficult at best since each partner must agree with what the other wants or else nothing changes. If there is no agreement, the local partner has a big edge because they are much more familiar with the local environment.

On the first trip when The Skooter goes with me, we are accompanied by my boss and his wife. Upon arrival, our Japanese counterparts want to know precisely when we are leaving. They are planning a schedule that includes a trip to Kyoto. Kyoto is known as the Imperial City and was largely spared from bombing. It is beautiful and revered by the Japanese. Interestingly, we Americans choose to stay overnight in a Japanese style inn and our Japanese friends pick a western style hotel. But we are all congenial and have a good time. No business is discussed until the final night when we are returning to Tokyo on the bullet train, which serves to emphasize Japan's current technical superiority.

We reach some agreements and arrive at our hotel late at night, knowing we have to leave for the airport at 5:30 AM. They say they will come by for breakfast and bring the typed agreement, but my boss says he doesn't want to get up that early and delegates the task to me. I am in the coffee shop when it opens and they present me a document about six pages long that some low-level employee must have stayed up all night to type. They show me the signature page but I decide to read it. I come to a part in the middle of the document which covers things we did not even talk about. Surprisingly, they agree.

I use this Japanese trip as a learning experience for whenever I have negotiations in various parts of the world. Always hold the negotiations in a place and atmosphere most favorable to you. For example, when I was responsible for a piece of a business in Guinea, West Africa I never went there. The country was run by reputed ruthless dictators, so I invited them to come to Washington. More importantly, when negotiating to get out of the venture, I suggested we meet in Paris, which they loved. I got everything I wanted in the agreement and their lawyers even bought a fancy lunch. It was a short lunch—they had other things they wanted to do.

(The Skooter, incidentally, thought I was crazy, missing chances for the adventure of going to Conakry, the capital of Guinea in West Africa.)

Another important point is to use time pressure in your favor. Always know when your negotiating counterpart has to leave for a plane, another appointment, or in one case, it was a very important suit fitting at Seville Row in London for the Norwegians' lawyer. It is amazing the number of unexpected concessions you can get when your negotiating counterpart is under tight time pressure and you are not.

But this is not a business book. It is about The Skooter and her insatiable desire for travel, particularly adventure travel.

We also travel all around Japan alone, and find the Japanese people most helpful and friendly. The Japanese are also very clean and keep things tidy and neat, in great contrast to much of China. I ask some of my friends why that is, and the best they can come up with is that, perhaps, it is because they are islands, and people that historically live on islands tend to be more tidy.

The Japanese also are extremely polite and avoid the word "no". They are so polite that it is difficult at times to know what they are really thinking. The Skooter and I stop at a good restaurant for lunch and she becomes enamored with a hand-carved bear from one of the northern islands. She tells me she wants to buy it. I tell her they won't sell it you; it is a treasure of the restaurant; and, furthermore, they won't say no to you. I don't think they have that word in their language. This makes her all the more determined to buy and she talks with several layers of management with her best smile and most convincing sales pitch. Finally, I get her to leave, and she mumbles that she couldn't even get them to give her a price. All they did was smile politely but they never said no.

We have many other interesting experiences with the Japanese. At one small town I stop to get a beer, but all that is there is a vending machine. All I have are some big yen bills. The machine says it will provide change and it is much bigger and more sophisticated than any we have in the U.S., so I trust it. I do get my beer but no change. I am about to chalk it up to experience and memories of a very expensive beer when a little man comes running out of a nearby house, apologizing profusely, and gives me my change from his pocket. When automation fails, the human hand is right there. What service!

The Japanese like pomp and ceremony and regular customary routine. Their women do not participate much in business, but when we have a business reception with wives, it is all very elegant and the women look terrific in their very best kimonos. We get a laugh when my Japanese counterpart who is very short, and I very tall, have to jockey the microphone up and down when making our ceremonial remarks. I think the party should be over, it has been a long evening, but no one leaves. Finally I get the word that no one will leave until the guests of honor, The Skooter and I, leave. It is probably the only party in her life where The Skooter was the first to leave.

The Skooter and I go to Nagasaki and spend a lot of time at the museum there. The devastation from the nuclear bomb is tragic and hard to believe. We hope the weapon is never used again. As we go around Japan though, we are struck by what natural fortresses these islands are, and we are told they were ready and waiting for our invasion. Cliffs go right down to the sea and we see few beaches. I was in the Marine Corps so I would have been there if we hadn't taken the nuclear option. The casualties would have been enormous.

In the U.S., we also have many interesting experiences when our Japanese partners visit. The Japanese love golf, so we try to accommodate. Of course, we have to provide the equipment. We get some of our employees to bring in their golf clubs to lend to the Japanese and put them in a room. But when the Japanese go in to select their clubs, they take one or two from each bag as if they are doing some sort of consumer test. Later, we have a very difficult time getting the clubs back to their rightful owners. After nine holes, my Japanese golfing partner disappears. I find him walking back to the clubhouse. He has lost all the golf balls I gave him and is too embarrassed to tell me.

The Japanese at our meetings in the U.S. are not big contributors in what are intended to be discussion sessions. They sit there with their eyes closed—asleep? No one challenges them—are we too polite? In one meeting, they particularly annoy me. We have a full meeting of non-participation, then a golf game, then a banquet with more closed eyes and at 10 P.M., they ask me what is next on the program. I simply tell them that I am going home to get some sleep.

The Japanese gain a world-wide reputation for engineering and technical expertise. They are ahead of us in many areas, such as trains, autos, etc., and the ability to manufacture with robots etc. This led to our second joint venture, since we had a business in California badly in need of refreshing. We thought they had the technical skills to help, as well as the marketing skills to expand our sales in Asia. It didn't work for many reasons I will not try to analyze here. Our Japanese partner was a company seeped in the past. When I go to visit in Tokyo [without The Skooter] I am struck with just how structured and rigid the company is. Their offices are in a big building overlooking the Imperial Palace. The executive dining room is on the top floor, very sumptuous and of course with a fabulous view of the Palace and Tokyo. When we go to the huge garage in the lower levels there are more black company limos than I have seen in any one location in the world. Must be quite a valued perk!

Chapter 29

New Zealand, Australia, Tasmania—Great Places to Visit

I cannot end this book without covering some of the best vacationing islands in the world. The Skooter and I loved them all and went as often as we could. These islands were some of the last places explored and settled by Europeans. The Dutch explorer, Tasman, is credited with being the first to sight New Zealand in 1642. On that same voyage, Tasman discovered Tasmania, an island south of Australia. Most of the early exploration activity and trading was to the north of Australia

Sydney Opera House

and I suspect that Tasman was the first to go around to the south and risk the ferocious storms that can come out of the Antarctic. The Skooter and I experienced one of those storms and that was enough. I thought the little ship was going to roll over and tried to crawl on my hands and knees up to the pilot house to find out what was happening. All ended well but our friends never went on another trip with us.

The Maori's were the early settlers in New Zealand and descendants are well taken care of by the government. Captain James Cook from England is revered as the explorer who put New Zealand on the map. His first voyage was in 1769. He not only mapped New Zealand but also the east coast of Australia and established England's claim to both countries. Reputedly New Zealand had no native animals, but when the first ships came they brought rats. To counteract this, weasels were imported but now they have trouble controlling the weasels. The first settlers found New Zealand well suited to farming, particularly for dairy products and sheep. Today there are many more sheep than people. The visit to a large sheep ranch that The Skooter and I make is a delight. Watching how they have trained their dogs to handle the sheep is a marvel. Another delight on the South Island is, in our minds, the best rain forest in the world, just great for hiking.

I was fortunate when attending Harvard Business School Advanced Management Program that one of my roommates was from New Zealand. Years later, we did reciprocal visits. The Skooter and I were awed by New Zealand. For us it was like going back in time, and I mean that in a positive way—back when life was simpler, the environment cleaner, etc. He had been president of a carpet company and when he retired he became Defense Minister of New Zealand. Later he became a health minister. Entering politics and running for office in New Zealand is relatively easy and inexpensive. They lived in Auckland and took us to their cottage north of Auckland on the ocean, high on a cliff overlooking the beach. The whole area was spectacular, but simple, no mansions. It reminded us of what the California coast must have looked like before we were born. The food and wine were excellent.

When our New Zealand friends came to Washington, we felt we had to give them a concentrated dose of politics, among other things. They were always asking why I didn't run for Congress and I just said you will see—lots of reasons. We started our morning on the Senate floor where a Senator was giving a speech on a very important subject—health care—to an audience of zero. I think they were stunned. Then we went to The Senate dining room for lunch and it was jammed with people, including many familiar Senators. After lunch we went to The House where someone was giving a speech that didn't make sense at all. A few people were on the floor in small groups but no one was even trying to listen to what the speaker was ranting about. I think our friends got the message that our Congress was bordering on the dysfunctional, without my ever having to say it. They never asked again why I didn't run for public office.

I could go on and on about the splendors of New Zealand, but this is a highlight book so The Skooter and I just urge you to go see for yourself. Australia is right next door. Sydney is one of the most beautiful cities in the world. Right on the ocean, you can live on the beach and take the ferry to work. But Australia is big and it has Darwin in the north, Perth in the west and Melbourne in the south. Most of the people live on the coast but there are attractions all over the country. I always admired the long stretches of beach running north of Sydney to the Great Barrier Reef, but when we get a good opportunity to explore it all, we are a little disappointed. Brisbane is at the end of a river, not on the ocean, and we were so spoiled by the sensational snorkeling on Bora Bora, that it ruined us for snorkeling anywhere else in the world.

The Dutch explorer, Willem Janszoon, is credited with the first sighting of Australia in 1606, but the British made the first settlements in the late 18th century. The first British penal colony was established in 1788 in New South Wales. Melbourne is the city that has retained a lot of old British charm, as well as good theater, but of course it is hard to top the spectacular Sydney Opera House. And Australia has enough in the way of native animals to enthrall The Skooter: the cuddly koala bears, but even more so, the friendly kangaroos of all sizes, who will eat right out of your hand.

Little Tasmania has only about 500,000 people but it is where the Aussies go to vacation so the Skooter and I had to find out what it is all about. It has just about everything you could want except luxury hotels. 45% of the land is held in reserves or parks. So there are lots of places to hike and camp out, mountains and beaches, and plenty of good food and wine. Tasmania was named after the Dutch explorer as I noted above, but became a British colony added to Australia. The only wild life we see is the Tasmanian Devil, who is not a very likable fellow with a nasty bite.

Chapter 30

The End

The Skooter had always wanted to go to Libya, mainly I think because she could not, and she thought the whole world, good and bad, should be hers to explore. So when Libya opened up, she signs us up. Unfortunately when we get there, Kaddafi decides that Americans cannot come ashore, so we end up with another trip around the Mediterranean, ending in Malta. But something very unusual happens in Malta. The Skooter gets very sick. When we get home, she goes to her doctor and he puts her in the hospital.

At first it appears to be something simple, like gall bladder, but no such luck. We get an evening call from a strange doctor we have never met saying The Skooter has pancreatic cancer and needs Whipple surgery, where they take out your pancreas and gall bladder, plus part of the stomach and intestine, and do some re-plumbing.

Son Brad hops right on it and says this is serious surgery, and if she has to have it, he is going to find the best with lots of experience. The surgery goes smoothly, but lasts seven hours, so it is a long wait. The doctor says it went well, but the cancer has spread to seven of the sixteen lymph glands he examined. Not exactly good news, but he also says it is a relatively non-aggressive type.

The Skooter makes a remarkably fast recovery, and quickly wants to resume all her many activities. No radiation or chemo for her. She throws herself into more extensive travel planning than ever. When she goes for her check-ups, she wants to talk about travel not her treatment. She gets all her doctors enthused about travel to remote places while I try to keep up with what she should do for treatment. Along the way, I find out that Steve Jobs has the exact same kind of cancer as The Skooter, His treatment is hard to follow, but there is no doubt about the very brilliant work he does while sick.

I cannot keep up with The Skooter on her travels. She wants to go to Kashmir and Srinagar to rent a houseboat, just like the days of the Raj. My research is not optimistic. There is a low-grade war going on between Pakistan and India, both of whom want to control Kashmir, and Srinagar is the epicenter. Furthermore, the houseboats look old and not very comfortable for someone as tall as I. All I can visualize is getting stuck on the lake in a leaky old houseboat and not being able to get off in Srinagar because of the shooting. So I am very happy when she finds two friends to head off with her on this adventure.

Unfortunately, or maybe fortunately, they never make it to Kashmir; the border is closed because of the fighting. They do have an adventure, however. They go up on the highest highway in the world and are hit by a snowstorm at 20,000 ft. The van has no oxygen but they are able to turn around and not get stuck. Before leaving India, The Skooter travels

On the road to Kashmir

The Skooter in Gabon

to New Delhi to visit a friend at the American Embassy and protest the border closing. Being shut out of Libya and now Kashmir is too much for her freedom of travel spirit.

As the Skooter shrinks, down to less than 90 pounds, her spirit for more travel continues to grow. Now she has picked out Gabon as her focus. She has read about an explorer who walked across The Congo and Gabon barefooted and then convinced the ruler of Gabon to establish a whole bunch of wildlife parks. I use all sorts of reasoning to talk her out of this one, without success. To me anyone that would walk across all that jungle has to be at least slightly crazy. The parks are not yet established. Gabon is heavily forested so, even though there are a lot of elephants, they hide in the forest, and you will never see them, etc.

For the first time she cannot find friends to go with her, so I am reduced to shouldn't, mustn't, and even can't — to no avail. I know I can't make it; my legs, etc., are showing their age. So I am reduced to finding her the best first class flights in and out, which isn't easy because there are so few flights. I book her through Morocco and back through Paris, after obtaining her solemn pledge not to leave the airport in Morocco seeking any adventure. And then I pray.

She makes it back and unloads on me. The trip was a disaster, but I have learned enough in a long, happy marriage to forego the "I told you so". I am just happy to have her back.

Forest Elephant in Gabon

I convince her to undertake something more placid for our next trip. The Skooter and I take a luxury cruise to the Norwegian fiords. After that, the Florida Dresslers invite the whole family for our 60th wedding anniversary celebration and Christmas. It is truly a wonderful get-together, and The Skooter and I enjoy it immensely. Little did we know it would be her last family vacation. We even had a professional photographer, so we have lots of great pictures to record the occasion.

The Skooter insists we must go to Machu Picchu, high in the mountains of Peru. I try to make it as easy a trip for her as possible, knowing it might be her last. We take a luxury cruise to Ecuador, fly to Lima, Peru, and stay overnight there. We have a late dinner and don't get to bed till almost midnight. The wake-up call is at 5 A.M. the next morning, so we can fly to Cusco. From Cusco we take a trip into the countryside to a llama farm and The Skooter is in her glory with all those lovable animals. It is difficult to get her out of the baby llama sweater store, but we do move on to a ranch for a delightful picnic lunch and then a demonstration of Spanish horseback riding and flamenco dancing.

When we finally get to our lovely quarters I am running on adrenalin and The Skooter collapses on a bed and passes out. I am thinking this is the end of this trip. Our guide tells us we can have room service for dinner, so I try to wake up The Skooter to tell her we can't go on with the trip unless she eats something, which she does, and goes right back to sleep.

The next morning I am hoping for the best, but maybe expecting the worst. But The Skooter hops out of bed and is ready to go, in better shape than I am. So it is on to Machu Picchu. The valley where the Incas lived runs between Cusco and Machu Picchu and has a river and rich soil. The Incas were said to have raised twenty-two different varieties of corn, one with kernels the size of your fingernail. Machu Picchu is built in the jungle on the side of a mountain. It is an engineering marvel for its stonework and drainage. Since it rains 90% of the time, without the proper drainage, the ledges where the people and animals lived would have been washed away long ago. We take the train and have a good lunch on it. The train gets you to a village close to the site. From there it is all uphill. No one knows why the Incas built this site in the jungle on the edge of their civilization. Did it have deep religious significance to them? Or some other purpose?

We get to the site in mid-afternoon and, amazingly, it is not raining but is somewhat warm—as good as the weather gets in Machu Picchu. I have purchased a wooden staff to help me with my weak knees. If it were raining, the stones would be a lot more slippery. The Skooter and I head out and around and down and up. It is truly remarkable what the Incas have built here. Why? Finally I tell The Skooter that I have had enough and have to go back, sit down and get some ice tea. But she is acting like a rejuvenated teen-ager and says she has to go on to the top. And she does.

We get to the train, have a nice dinner but no drinks. Alcohol and high altitude don't mix very well. But many are celebrating with the local rum drink when the train comes to a screeching halt. We have no idea what has happened, but it looks like another late night. The Skooter is lively enough to go to the club car while we wait it out. Finally, we get moving again and make it to our beautiful hotel, converted from a monastery, about 1:00 A.M. I crash and look forward to sleeping in. When I do wake up about 8:30 A.M., The Skooter is gone. She has gone into downtown Cusco for more exploring.

We have a quiet last day in Cusco. I take what turns out to be the very last photo of The Skooter, but it is very symbolic. She is very happy,

Last ever photo of The Skooter, in Cusco on Machu Pichu trip

sitting with two brightly dressed Peruvian women and holding a baby llama in her arms.

We journey onward to Chile, which we enjoy very much. Then home on a long overnight flight. The Skooter had agreed with her doctors to try a new chemo drug when she finishes this trip. We learn that Steve Jobs has gone to Tennessee to get a liver transplant, but we are told that The Skooter is not eligible because her cancer has spread. Actually it doesn't do that much to extend his life beyond hers.

The Skooter had never really wanted to talk about death because she had so much living she still wanted to do. After three sons and five grandsons, she knew a granddaughter was on the way. She had told me that she wanted to be buried in Cleveland where she was born. Although an Episcopalian all her life, she did not want a formal funeral, but rather a rejoicing for friends and family and not one, but two: one in Cleveland and one in Washington D.C.

As I mentioned in an earlier chapter, several years before, in Newport, R.I., we had purchased a full-sized bronze lion. We had him shipped to Washington and set-up to guard our front door. I asked her if she wanted something like that as a grave marker to show her love of animals and guard her until I got there. She thought that was a good idea, but first she wanted to take me on a special tour to see all the grandeurs of India, see her new granddaughter, etc.

And then very suddenly, everything came unglued. I had a bad fall in a parking lot outside of Baltimore. They took me to a hospital in Columbia, MD and I was diagnosed with a pelvis broken in two places and a crushed elbow. That night they operated to wire my elbow back together. David Jr. came from California and Brad from Florida. It was so terrific how they both rose to the emergency situation. Then The Skooter had a fall at home and was taken to the hospital. The wire in my elbow broke and I had to have another operation to put a cable in. We ended up in the hospital in rooms four doors apart, but I was told she was in respite care.

Those were the toughest days of my life. Seeing "the love of my life" slowly wasting away and not being able to do anything about it tore me apart. I was in great physical pain but the emotional stress was almost unbearable. My support team of long-term employees, Romeo and Enid, really helped pull me through.

Sons, David Jr. and Brad were so supportive all the way. They carried the burden of making what we now call The Lion Memorial, a reality. The spot picked for it is just so beautiful, in the woods next to a canyon and well separated from everything except for nature, just as The Skooter would want it. We had an Episcopal minister for final family only services at the gravesite, and then the rejoicings for friends, just as The Skooter wanted.

For those of you who thought this was just a travel book, you now know it is also very much a love story. Our love will go on forever.

The End

the end—
it will always come
not now—I have so much still to do
the end—
it will always come why—when—how
you will never know
did you know when you were born why—when—how
you will never know
when you least expect it when you least want it
the end—
it will always come

transmitted by The Skooter 2 AM, January 30, 2014

The Skooter Gets to Critique This Book

Question: Hey Skooter, how do you think I did in depicting your adventure travels and endless energy?

Answer: Well you did a pretty good job but you left so much out.

Response: I know, but if I covered everything it would be so long no one would read it. I did short change the USA where I think we covered every state with some sort of trip. There are so many great places to vacation right here in the USA. And Canada where the areas and provinces are so different and give such a variety of travel experiences. Quebec so French.

Question: Hey Skooter, what funny experiences did I miss?

Answer: A lot. Our trip to Cairo when you decided you would become an Arab with a beard and long robes so we could go anywhere, including afternoon prayers. Of course, you had me, a blonde as your companion, so you told me I should learn a few words of Swedish for the sake of safety. The pyramids and Luxor were awesome. You ended up drinking the

Nile River water because you were constipated. And don't forget how shocked you were in India when I wrapped the live cobra around my neck.

Question: Skooter, what areas of beauty did you like that I missed?

Answer: The fabulous botanical gardens all over the world. Singapore was picture perfect in every way and had one of the best. But Wellington, New Zealand, rivaled London, and the British Embassy in Washington for roses. And the botanical gardens in Johannesburg were very special.

Question: The world is always changing. We saw an awful lot of it, for better and worse. Dave, as a Phi Beta Kappa major in Economics and Psychology from Yale, what was the single biggest positive change we observed?

Answer: The emergence of entrepreneurship in Eastern Europe when the old Iron Curtain crumbled. The people's spirit had not been destroyed. Just one very small example: When we first went to Prague and walked down a desolate street, a man had opened the window to his house and was selling Belgium waffles he made on the spot, with chocolate sauce and whipped cream. They were so delicious he quickly sold out. Then he closed the window and went back in his kitchen to whip up more batter. A one-man operation giving the people something new that they didn't even know they wanted or needed.

Question: Hey, Skooter, you loved all the people of the world. It must be pretty hard on you what is happening in the Muslim world.

Answer: Indeed it is. Remember when our Harvard Professor, Ali, gave us those educational lectures on Islam? It is a beautiful religion and

Petra

doesn't deserve to be torn into factions of hate. Remember how much fun we had in Uzbekistan and how we admired how they had built the first observatory in the world? Islam is not a religion of killing and hate. My firm wish is that the world comes together in love and respect for others.

Question: Skooter, any last thought of awesome beauty I left out of the book?

Answer: Yes, you didn't mention going to Iguazu Falls before the dam was built between Brazil, Argentina and Paraguay. We walked from Brazil to Argentina over a rickety wooden bridge over the onrushing water in a totally unspoiled jungle atmosphere. Also, when we went through the narrow, rocky passage that served as the entrance to the hidden city of Petra in Jordan. It was so spectacular when we first viewed the city itself, which had been carved out of stone long ago. We got to do lots of climbing around that ancient marvel that everyone should visit.

One final question: Skooter: Did you ever feel you had to rely on those guardian angels on each shoulder to save you when you charged ahead into the unknown?

Answer: Not really, I always had you, and we had each other's back when we were traveling.

Response: Yes, Skooter. You never hesitated to save and love your man. You have had and will have my undying love forever. I miss you so much.

About David and Skooter Dressler

David C. Dressler graduated from Shaker Heights High School in Ohio in 1946. He graduated from Yale University in 1950 as a Phi Beta Kappa in Economics and Psychology. While at Yale he joined the U.S. Marine Corps Reserve. He served on active duty from 1951 to 1953, rising to the rank of Captain. He married Dorothea "Skooter" Walker in December 1950. In 1953, David joined Master Builders, which became a division of Martin Marietta Corp. He rose through the ranks to become President. Subsequently, in Bethesda, MD he became President of Chemicals, Materials, and Aluminum, as well as Senior Vice President of Martin Marietta Corp. In various positions, he did business all over the world, directly or through joint ventures. He retired from what is now Lockheed Martin in 1992.

Dorothea "Skooter" Walker graduated from Shaker Heights High School in 1947 and Colby-Sawyer College in New London, NH in 1949. Following marriage to David, she had 3 sons, two of whom graduated from Yale. The third was severely handicapped from birth and she raised him at home until he was in his 30's. She was always very active in charity work wherever she lived. Known for her great energy, she managed to balance family, charity work, her love of animals, and of course, travel until her death from pancreatic cancer in 2011

CPSIA information can be obtained at www.ICGtesting.com
Printed in the USA
BVIW12n1115120816
458145BV00004B/1